Bobcat Year

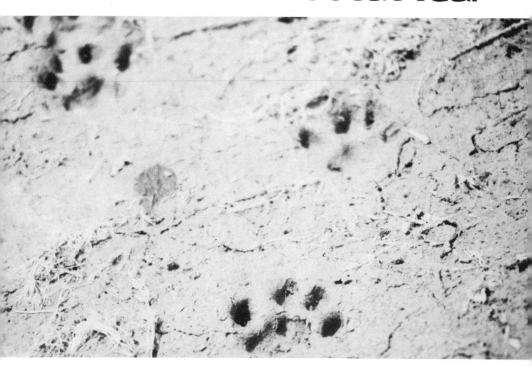

Text and Photographs by
HOPE RYDEN

Bobcat
Year

LYONS & BURFORD,
PUBLISHERS

In loving memory of my father,

whose pleasure in language became my own

LIBRARY OF CONGRESS CATALOGING-IN-PUBLICATION DATA

Ryden, Hope.
Bobcat year : text and photographs / Hope Ryden.
p. cm.
Reprint. Originally published: New York : Viking Press, 1981.
Includes bibliographical references (p.).
ISBN 1-55821-055-5 : $14.95
1. Bobcat.   I. Title.
[QL737.C23R92   1990]
599.74'428—dc20   90-31920
CIP

Printed in the United States of America

10   9   8   7   6   5   4   3   2   1

Contents

Introduction by Roger A. Caras   ix

SPRING   3

SUMMER   49

FALL   109

WINTER   145

Author's Note   195

    A Bobcat Update—1990   197

    Sources   203

Acknowledgments

While studying bobcats in Arizona, Idaho, California, and Florida, I was given help, direction, and hospitality by a variety of people and organizations and am indebted to many more than I can name. In singling out a few, I hope that those I fail to mention will forgive me. In Arizona, personnel at the Arizona Sonora Desert Museum aided me in every conceivable way, and I am particularly grateful to those administrators who granted me permission to make round-the-clock observations of the museum's bobcats. Ranchers in Arizona were consistently willing to help me. Claude McNair spent considerable time with me scouting bobcat signs, and rancher Don McEwen invited me to make use of his land as a study site. Defenders of Wildlife assisted me in many ways, not the least of which was to grant me use of its Arizona property in Aravaipa Canyon and its Wildlife Preserve near Oracle. Maxine Guy of Tubac, who is licensed by the Arizona Department of Fish and Game to rehabilitate injured and orphaned wildlife, not only extended hospitality to me but also made it possible for me to make close-range observations of the animals in her care. I also wish to thank Arizona University graduate student David Lawhead for inviting me to accompany him to the Three Bar Wildlife Area in the Tonto National Forest, where he was completing a sixteen-month telemetry study on bobcats. Bob Davison, a wildlife cinematographer from Utah, graciously allowed me to be present while he filmed a television documentary on desert flora and fauna in which his own trained bobcat performed. Bob's understanding of natural history and his way with animals was a joy to observe, and I am indebted to him for introducing me to his fifteen-year-old bobcat, Prince. In Idaho I was received with similar enthusiasm and offered help from every quarter. Personnel at the National Engineering Laboratory near Arco were entirely supportive of my efforts to locate bobcats on that 640-square-kilometer nuclear testing station. And when I searched areas outside of that high-security site, local people went out of their way to direct me to possible bobcat habitats. Californians, too, offered me every kind of assistance. Paula and Carl Guthrie shared with me detailed information on the orphaned bobcat they had reared and were about to release into the wild. Carol and Oscar Hills offered me quarters on their beautiful wild property in the Inland Coastal Range. In Florida, I received the same wonderful treatment. Dr. James Layne, director of biological research for the American Museum of Natural History, permitted me to track bobcats on the museum's Archbold Biological Research Station near Lake Placid. Another bobcat watcher working there, Ph.D. candidate Douglas Wassmer, invited me to travel with him while he monitored radio signals from his collared subjects. And residents of the station, Marsha and Chet Winegarten, allowed me to make observations of a bobcat they had reared and released some years earlier. The animal still made periodic visits to their backyard. Even in New York City live people with special knowledge of bobcats. Former animal trainer Jacque Dean and her husband, Dr. Irv Rinard, shared with me their vast experience and knowledge of wildcats. Perhaps I owe most to biologist Dr. Theodore Bailey and German ethologist Dr. Paul Leyhausen for their peerless studies of cats. I was privileged to meet both of them, and though our conversations were too brief, their published research served as a guide to me and helped me understand and interpret the cat behavior I was observing. A special thanks is owed to photographer Dick Randall, whose picture of a trapped bobcat appears on page 192 of this book. Dick's efforts to alert the public to the cruelty of trapping springs from firsthand knowledge. It was while Dick was employed as a government trapper that he became sensitive to the impact of the leghold trap on wild animals. The two charming kittens featured on page 11 were taken by Leonard Lee Rue III. I was grateful to locate these pictures, one of which perfectly answered an "age gap" I was unable to illustrate with my own photography. Finally, I would like to thank my editor at The Viking Press, Barbara Burn, for her enthusiastic support of this project, her sound guidance, and her sensitivity to animals.

Introduction

There are animals few of us ever get to see in the wild much less know as individuals. They are special for that if for no other reason. They don't stand by the side of the road and they don't come to our bird feeders or garbage pails. No animals are more cryptic and reclusive than the usually nocturnal, always shy and retiring bobcats. You can spend a life-time nature watching and never see any member of the lynx group outside of a museum, zoo or, heaven help us, fur salon. Those we see on television in nature specials are *almost* always captive and trained animals.

But there are people who have a combination of skills, love and understanding who do get to know the elusive ones. They don't use dart guns or traps and they don't hunt with anything more deadly than their cameras and their binoculars. We depend on them to go out into the wild places for us, use their finely honed patience and skills and see what so few of us ever see. Then they report back to us and say, "This is what you have. Guard it, cast out those among us who won't."

Hope Ryden, whether her target is the feral or "wild" horse of the American West, the coyote, beaver or the bobcat is such a special category observer and reporter. The best part of it is Ms Ryden is not only a skilled wildlife observer and nature photographer she is an enchanting writer. Her years as a television producer trained her to construct well-reasoned stories and reports without waste and frills. Her artistry picks up from that point and she creates prose that is at once gripping and instructive. She is, in fact, in the view of anyone who has studied and cared about our wild places and wild things, a kind of national treasure.

I am sure Ms Ryden is realistic about the terrible problems the bobcat faces and the dreary prognosis that one could construct from present trends and the evidence at hand. But like any true conservationist and wildlife supporter she knows there is absolutely no future in pessimism. Optimism is the only available alternative but optimism requires (and certainly deserves) our real support and devotion. People support what they know and are devoted to that which they love. That is where the rare Hope Rydens of the world come in. They help us to know, to understand and they guide us to where we can care, i.e. love.

The bobcat is a special animal of this continent. Its relatives like the Canadian lynx, the African serval, the caracal of India, the Middle East and Africa and the other increasingly rare smaller cats worldwide are worth saving. That is true, of course, of all wild animals and plants but the predators have been so severely harassed because of inexplicable prejudice (could it be jealousy?) and because of their fur that they somehow seem special. To a purist that may not be true, but we are not required to be purists all of the time.

Bobcat Year belongs on every nature lover's shelf be they the most austere, arcane scientific type or just another little old lady in dirty white tennis shoes. It certainly belongs in the hands of every young person, those who can read and those who are still being read to. They, after all, possess the future, a future the likes of Hope Ryden are trying to make just as good as it can be. It wouldn't be all that good in North America without the bobcat.

—ROGER CARAS
THISTLE HILL FARM
FREELAND, MARYLAND

SPRING

Chapter 1

The kitten tapped the dark water with his paw and watched the dim reflection of his face dissolve. When the ripples subsided and a bobcat image resolved itself anew on the surface of the pool, he swatted the enemy again. Then, tiring of the game, he licked the water from his round paws and, in a few unsteady bounds, joined his mother on the bank.

His sister had been hiding behind a rock, waiting for something to ambush. Now, as the male kitten lit, she pounced, and the chase that ensued led the pair into tall sedge. Though they were now hidden from view, the eyes of the mother cat tracked the wake that her babies created as they charged about in the vegetation. After a while she arose and located them. With a swipe of her tongue, she bowled the male kitten onto his back and proceeded to clean him vigorously.

The young bobcat submitted to the rhythmic massage of his mother's tongue, which caused his heart rate to slow and his brain-wave pattern to shift to a more measured pace. These changes were sensed by the young kitten as pleasurable.

Meanwhile his sister, eyeing her mother's twitching tail, crouched and sprang. But the mother cat was alert, and she caught her offspring in mid-leap, toppled her, and began to clean this, her other surviving kitten. The baby closed her greening eyes and abandoned herself to the bliss of being groomed.

Three kittens had been born to the wild mother cat, but a disturbance had interrupted the birth process shortly after the first baby had been successfully delivered. Footfalls had reverberated in the bobcat's rock shelter, and the smell of horses had permeated the darkness of the natal den. Finally, human chatter had activated the

3

female bobcat's adrenal system and all birth contractions had ceased.

The two rock hunters who scaled the pile of boulders that morning were in high spirits. While their tethered horses stomped and snorted, the young man and woman clambered about on the big stones, creating minor avalanches where they moved. Pleased to be spending a spring day in this wild Idaho desert, the two felt exhilarated, at one with nature. They would have been surprised at the impact their presence was having on an animal but a few feet away.

The natal den had been carefully chosen and casually prepared by the pregnant cat. It was not so much a cave as a space that existed between the huge boulders which lay at the base of a glacial moraine. The entrance to this cavity was a narrow fissure. Outside, planted like warning flags to alert the bobcat world that the site was claimed, were several scat mounds. Inside the barren cavity, grass had been raked about. This nesting material, carried in by the bobcat, was not of sufficient quantity to pad the floor; so scantly was it scattered, in fact, that it appeared to serve no function at all. Perhaps it did not. Perhaps it was a ritualized expression of some once purposeful nest-building activity carried out in ages past by one of the cat's remote ancestors, the tree-dwelling miacids. On the other hand, this bobcat may simply have been interrupted by the sudden onset of labor before completing her natal preparations.

When contractions began to occur at frequent intervals, the female made use of the grass, scraping it from one side of the rock cavity to the other. Performing such movements helped relieve the terrible pains that wracked her body and, at one moment, even caused her to emit an uncharacteristic mew. As a result, in the end, all the shredded chaff lay heaped in one corner, where it failed to soften the firstborn kitten's initial contact with a hard world.

At the moment her water broke, the female cat quickly and vigorously licked her vaginal region, and a male kitten was delivered. Swiftly, the mother bobcat identified the baby as hers and proceeded to separate him from the placental material to which he was attached. Not until the newborn had been thoroughly washed and was squalling did she examine the iron-rich membranous matter that had been the kitten's life support in the womb. This she ingested, and by so doing, she accomplished two ends. First, she cleaned her kitten's living quarters, making it a fit nursery. At the same time, she availed herself of highly nutritious food. Thus fed,

she would not be driven by hunger to take leave of her young to hunt for at least a day or two. She needed this time to recover from the strenuous effort of giving birth.

A lurch in her uterus signaled that a second kitten was about to descend into the birth canal. The mother responded to the sharp pain by circling, but the contractions only grew more intense. Again she tried to gain relief by clawing at the cave floor and panting. But her second baby, whose birth seemed so imminent, was not destined to be delivered for several hours. Parturition could not proceed except in absolute privacy, and human beings had approached paralyzingly near to the bobcat's den.

In actual fact, the terror-stricken animal was in little danger of being discovered. The young people's perception of their surroundings was limited by their own single-minded aim to find arrowheads and gemstones, and the interstitial places where life hides did not touch upon their solid-world consciousness. Even a green and brown rattlesnake, lying fully extended in a cool crevice, failed to capture their attention.

The animals were not so oblivious. The bobcat sensed the proximity of the two human beings even before their sounds and scents wafted through the chink of light that was the entrance to her birthing chamber. Instantly, the limbic portion of her brain signaled her body to take flight. But the impulse was countermanded. For though the rock hunters were finding little to pocket, they were nevertheless in no hurry to leave the elephantine boulders upon which they slipped and perched. And because the bobcat, a reclusive and wary creature, dared not reveal herself, both she and her unborn kitten were condemned to wait, to remain inert, until the two human beings at last mounted their horses and departed.

Even after they had left, the high-strung bobcat did not quickly recover from the stress she had suffered, and she could not immediately resume the business of bearing young. When at last she did begin to grow calm, a smoldering cigarette butt dropped near the entrance to her rock chamber suddenly flared up, once again setting off her panic. In a frenzy, she abandoned the den. Streaking eastward, she headed for another rock outcropping, one that overlooked a streambed where she sometimes hunted. In her mouth she carried one protesting kitten. In her belly she carried two.

The baby's loud, high-pitched squalls, as he swung from her jaws, failed to incite the usual response in the mother cat. Ordinarily, such birdlike sounds would have released in her a sequence of predatory actions that would terminate in the killing of prey. But today no such behavior was elicited, and the vulnerable infant was carried in a soft mouth. Maternity had temporarily inhibited the bobcat's hunting instincts. Thus nature safeguarded baby bobcats, preventing them from being confused with prey and destroyed.

The bobcat knew well the land she was crossing. It had been thoroughly explored and occupied by her since the untimely death of its former occupant, a young tom. Now her scat piles replaced his and were posted in conspicuous places along her travel routes and beside den sites. Routinely, she inspected and renewed these signs of her presence. By such means the solitary creature inadvertently reserved rabbits and resting places for her exclusive use and avoided unpleasant encounters with strangers. Any transient bobcat who might stray onto this five-square-mile home range would not linger long. No less than the resident female, the stranger would also be a seeker of privacy.

But the streambed toward which she now hurried posed a different situation. Water, being scarce throughout Idaho's high desert, was a resource that was shared by many bobcats, wherever it happened to be found. Thus the stream was sometimes visited by animals whose own home ranges stood at some distance. Their use of the place was evident from the variety and number of paw prints which intermingled on the stream bank. Yet actual encounters between thirsty members of the species *Lynx rufus* rarely occurred. Except during mating season, the reclusive felines hid themselves from one another or staggered their trips to drink.

Now the female bobcat headed for a den, a high cave that overlooked this watering place. She knew the cliff wall well, having dragged many a rabbit carcass into its high recesses, places beyond the reach of coyotes, who might otherwise try to confiscate a hard-won dinner. Only another bobcat could scale the almost vertical precipices that rose on both sides of the stream for several miles, and another bobcat would not be likely to seek contact with one of its kind.

From above, the approach to this particular cave was even more treacherous than from below. It was located midway down the cliff, requiring a headlong descent in a series of precise and daring leaps. Even if she had not been handicapped by pregnancy and clenching a kitten in her mouth, such a maneuver would have been difficult. Yet the determined bobcat did not hesitate. Down the precipice she leaped. No intruders would discover this den.

Inside the cave, amid bone litter from past feasts, she dropped her shrieking kitten and, for a few minutes, watched the blind infant make futile swimming motions on the floor as it desperately tried to locate a teat. She made no move to assist the scrabbling infant. Her behavior was disordered, her maternal responses deranged. Not only was she exhausted from her half-mile trek, but what was happening inside her own body now demanded all her attention. Panting, she tried to lower herself to the ground, but the act of shifting her posture created stabbing pain inside her womb. One unborn kitten had become lodged in her birth canal, where it now blocked the passage of a third, ready-to-be-born fetus.

The bobcat hunkered down and strained. She panted and clawed and cried out. But she could not gain relief. For four hours she labored. Then, exhausted, she ceased to make efforts. Resignation clouded her eyes as she gave herself up to the inevitability of death.

On the floor where she lay, the importunate wails of her kitten sounded in her ears, but they failed to arouse her fading consciousness. When the kitten finally discovered a plucked breast, the unresponsive female did not rise up and shake him off.

The infant had nursed for less than two minutes when his inert mother was suddenly seized with violent contractions, raising her to her feet in a paroxysm of pain. In rapid succession, she expelled two fetuses. At first, the birth debris and the newborn young appeared to make no impression on the dazed bobcat. She made no move to peel away the transparent membrane that enveloped each baby. But the last-born kitten, struggling inside its cowl, at last attracted its mother's interest, and, in a desultory fashion, she began to lick away the sticky substance that imprisoned it. As she did so, the characteristic taste of the new offspring imprinted itself on her brain. And before the tiny creature was free, even before it had begun to vocalize, a bond was forged between mother and baby. This kitten, a female, was also recognized as the bobcat's own.

The remaining baby now attracted its mother's attention, and she proceeded to attend to it. But she did so in an irresolute manner, frequently turning her attention to the two who were nursing. Moreover, before she freed this kitten from the membrane that encased it, she took time to consume its attached placenta, thus further depriving the infant of access to oxygen.

When at last she did clean the birth fluid from its nose and mouth, the perfectly formed creature made no sound. The mother cat pushed at it with her nose, then observed closely as the baby slowly doubled back into a fetal position like a closing blossom. Though a spark of life still powered its tiny heart, she ceased to kindle it. Mysteriously, she had received another message from the brain-damaged creature. With exquisite gentleness, she picked it up and carried it out of the cave, took it to a place where its odd responses would not contaminate her two healthy kittens.

On the sunny cliff ledge where she left it, the infant died.

Chapter 2

The sun struck the western face of the cliff and warmed the rocks. The female bobcat moved to the entrance of her den and basked in its radiation. Her two kittens burrowed under her body. Their eyes, blue slits, admitted a blurry vision of the world now. The babies were developing rapidly. In two weeks' time their weight had doubled, and on this day their ear canals were opening; pulses of sound were registering in their brains. Until now the kittens had lived exclusively in a world of scent.

Their blindness and deafness had not, however, prevented the young kittens from exploring their surroundings. Their noses were exquisitely sensitive, and they navigated about their nest by following their own bodies' scent trails. Had they been removed from their den, deprived of their own odor traces, and placed in fresh surroundings, the babies' disorientation would have become obvious, their distress audible. Only amid familiar smells could they negotiate space and feel safe.

Two ducts situated in their upper gums and leading to a special sensor, the Jacobson's organ, enhanced the bobcats' ability to "read" with their noses, enabled them to plot routes across the stony floor. This nose adjunct even permitted them to locate a preferred nipple on their mother's body. So discriminating was their sense of smell, the babies would return to the same teats each time they nursed.

But today the kittens' world was opening wider. Light bombarded their eyes and sound vibrated in their unfolding ears. Distressed by so many new sensations, they wriggled under their mother's protective body and began kneading her scratched belly with their tiny forepaws. Milk, familiar milk, comforted them.

Although nursing could be accomplished quickly, the female bobcat spent much time tending her two kittens. She groomed them with care. With her rough tongue, coated with minute, hook-shaped papillae, she rasped away dust and debris that clung to their spotted coats. She attended to their bodily functions, licking their anal regions until the kittens defecated. Then she consumed the waste. In so doing, she kept her home free of flies and odors which otherwise might attract the attention of an enemy.

As for her own waste, that material she put to another use. Since moving to the cliff den, the female had not buried her stools, but repeatedly defecated on one or another of three conspicuous rocks. Eventually, these piles of scat became visible features along the cliff rim, like stones stacked by a surveyor. And like a surveyor's markers, her scat piles notified others of her claim, discouraging them from settling in the same area. Thus, inadvertently, the female reserved for her own use what cottontails bred in the immediate vicinity. While her kittens were young, it was important that she be able to hunt close to home.

In the days immediately following the traumatic birth of her litter, the mother cat had felt no impulse to hunt. The three placentas she had consumed had answered her nutritional needs. When the kittens were four days old, however, she suddenly experienced an urge to stalk prey, and she left her babies, ascended to the top of the cliff, and ambushed a young rabbit.

Uncharacteristically, she ate the kill where she felled it. Normally, she would have dragged the cottontail to some less conspicuous feeding site, but on this occasion, her impatience to return to her young did not permit her to indulge her passion for privacy. Nevertheless, after dining, she did take time to clean her forefeet and scrub her face thoroughly with a wet paw. Her fastidious nature was uncompromising, a behavioral trait that no doubt served the species by protecting her kittens and herself from bacterial infection.

The hunting foray could be counted a success inasmuch as the nourishment she obtained far exceeded what calories she had to expend to catch the rabbit. Her survival always depended on just such a cost-benefit balance. Especially now that nursing kittens were sapping her body's reserves, she could ill afford hunting failure.

When she returned to the den, her kittens smelled traces of rabbit on her breath and registered the impression. But, as yet, the infant carnivores had no appetite for flesh, no inkling of their top-of-the-food-chain destiny. Only their mother's milk, now flowing copiously, excited them, and, like every infant mammal, they found their way to her full teats with amazing ease.

Outside the bobcats' natal den, the offspring of other animals were making similar demands on their mothers. Black-tailed fawns waited in the willows for does to return from a day of browsing. Greedily they drank the rich milk their mothers' bodies had concocted for them. Great horned owls scooped rodents from the sedge that fringed the stream and carried them to their fledglings. A black raven discovered the decomposed body of the kittens' sibling and recycled it into ongoing raven life. Each morning a mother coyote lapped water from the stream, replacing the fluids her suckling pups had extracted from her body.

At night the bobcat listened to a pack of coyotes affirm their bonds in song. Their ululations ricocheted throughout the canyon, obscuring all clues as to the precise location of the sociable canids. The bobcat was of a different nature—silent and self-contained. Like an initiate to some high holy order, the female was capable of maintaining a single, unrelieved posture for long periods of time without growing languid or falling asleep. Her alertness was, in fact, remarkable. No scurrying mouse or camouflaged lizard escaped her attention. In particular, she was keenly aware of the presence of any bobcat who came to drink at the stream. Yet, while she observed these occasional visitors with obvious interest, she felt no impulse to make contact with any of them.

With her kittens she was a different animal. Not only did her young evoke her profoundest interest, they aroused in her states

which, when observed in human beings, are ordinarily described as affectionate or protective, even altruistic. The mother cat met any perceived threat to her offspring with selfless combativeness, the intensity of which far exceeded what her slight stature suggested possible. The proverbial "mother tiger," it would appear, could come in any size, and the female bobcat was a twenty-pound mother tiger.

When her kittens were three and a half weeks old, she demonstrated this maternal commitment to their survival by wrestling with a rattlesnake. Although bobcats and snakes had cohabited in the rocky cliffs since time immemorial, no real truce existed between the two animals. Sometimes a serpent would fall prey to a bobcat; more rarely, a bobcat kitten would serve as food for a serpent. Yet, despite their natural enmity, neither cat nor reptile had managed to displace the other from their mutually preferred habitat, nor had either caused the other's extinction.

Now that the female bobcat was guarding young, however, she was more than normally intolerant of snakes. Frequently, she scanned the dark walls of her cave home for a sign of their presence. But, as her babies grew more mobile, watching over them became increasingly difficult. Often the two kittens took off in opposite directions to explore different fissures in the rock walls. Some of the crevices they squeezed into were hardly wide enough to admit one kitten. At such times the mother bobcat, unable to follow where her offspring went, could do little more than call them back in a special voice reserved just for that purpose. But the kittens did not always obey.

The male, in particular, enjoyed running up a ramp that sloped along the rear wall of the cave. One day he encountered a rattlesnake lying outstretched at the top of that runway. The sight of the serpent did not alarm the kitten. On the contrary, the snake intrigued him. To the young bobcat, anything that moved was of interest and had to be investigated. Moreover, if the purpose of the snake's rattles was to warn away enemies, the kitten was not born with any knowledge of the fact. To him the whirring sound produced by the snake's segmented tail was no more menacing than were the wingbeats of a june bug or the rustle of dried leaves. With his paw he tried to catch the rapidly vibrating appendage. The snake began to coil.

The rattlesnake was sluggish. Only that morning it had devoured a small rabbit, and afterward it had glided into the cave to sleep off its huge unchewed meal. The process of converting an entire cottontail—fur, bone, muscle, organs—into pliable snake matter demanded much energy from the animal. Its fangs were hypodermic needles, useful only to inject victims with poison. They were neither of a shape nor sufficiently strong to masticate food. When the snake ate, it opened its hinged mouth improbably wide and ingested its prey whole. Afterward, it became a lethargic and unaggressive creature, not inclined to look for trouble with a baby bobcat.

But the rattlesnake's peace had been disturbed, and now it reacted defensively. With rapid darts of its forked tongue, it tested the air for stray molecules until the baby bobcat's presence was registered. Immediately, both ends of its long body came alive. While its tongue continued to flick at a moderate rate, its tail buzzed almost imperceptibly sixty times a second.

The male kitten crept closer, circled the partially coiled snake, and crouched. Poised to pounce, he waited for the right moment to leap upon the reptile's twelve alluring rattles. But on the cave floor below, the mother cat had heard a rasping sound and grown attentive. It was her baby's hiss, however, that brought her to life, raised her to her feet. In an imperious voice, one that her kittens had not heard before, she called.

Momentarily arrested by his mother's sharp tone, the male kitten aborted his pounce. He did not, however, obey her command to come down off the ledge. Perhaps a mellow chortle would have enticed him to descend, might have suggested to his infant mind that milk was flowing. But such a sound would have welled from a different mood than the one the mother cat was now experiencing. The excited call she now repeated again and again issued from a body that was readying itself to do battle.

The serpent, possessing no ears, heard nothing at all. Moreover, in the dim cave light, the reptile's eyesight was not sharp enough to pinpoint the kitten's precise whereabouts. Yet the snake possessed another sense, which operated with infallible accuracy. Two facial pits situated between its eyes and nostrils tingled with sensation. Radiation—heat produced by the warm-blooded kitten who had come into its presence—activated nerves in these pits and now enabled the snake to close in on its victim as unerringly as sonar plumbs dark water for sunken objects.

The reptile surged forward. Like a locomotive starting up, energy flowed through its long body a section at a time. By the time

its tail received the message to glide, the creature's head was already scanning the rock shelf, searching for space in which to turn. For by now the snake had taken a bearing on its target and was positioning itself to strike.

Both the bobcat and the rattlesnake were endowed by nature with physical characteristics and behavioral responses to serve them in such a circumstance. Yet the match between the two species was not an equal one. The snake was a mature animal, the bobcat an inexperienced kitten. The outcome of such an uneven contest was predictable.

Nevertheless, the kitten possessed one evolutionary asset that even yet could save him. In the mammalian world, young animals enjoy the protection of vigilant mothers. And at that very moment, fierce maternal help was on the way.

Ignoring the ramp, the mother cat clawed her way straight up the cave wall, and even before the reptile had sensed the presence of a second cat on the ledge, she grabbed it by the neck and her sharp fangs had penetrated deep into its rubbery flesh.

The snake writhed and thrashed. But the bobcat held on and dug into the hard rock with her sharp claws to stabilize herself against the force of the snake's wild convolutions.

The bobcat's entire physical system was galvanized for action.

Tenaciously, she maintained her grip and waited for the snake's powerful muscular action to subside. Her glazed eyes and steadfast expression gave no hint of her inner tension. Killing was a dangerous way of life that demanded her entire attention.

The snake did not die quickly. Even though mortally wounded, it continued to writhe and thrash and fight for its life. But at last its undulations began to subside, and the bobcat pressed its thick body to the floor with a paw and bit off its poisonous head. Yet even this did not put an end to the serpent's activity; for some time afterward, its headless body produced reflexive contractions. Finally, the female bobcat picked up these remains and dragged them down the ramp. Her kitten pranced after her.

On the floor of the cave, in view of her two babies, the mother bobcat made a meal of her adversary. Inside her victim, she discovered a windfall—the partially digested body of a young rabbit. Making up for past and future want, the bobcat gorged, eating snake and rabbit until she hurt. Many days and nights might pass before she would catch herself another such meal.

Chapter 3

At four weeks the kittens were irrepressible. They pawed and bit one another in mock combat. When one kitten's interest in a game began to flag, the other would roll onto its back and solicit more play. Their movements were spasmodic. After one or two bounds, a kitten might come to a teetering halt and await the signal from its brain that would once again propel its body forward. When the connection was restored, the baby would be jolted into another spurt of activity.

With an air of complacency, the mother cat observed her young at play. But on occasion she could not resist joining in their high jinks. Her abbreviated tail intrigued her offspring, and she sometimes twitched it just to stir up their excitement. The kittens would leap upon it repeatedly, as if subduing some formidable enemy. When the wriggling stump slipped from their clasp, they would tumble to the ground.

Her stubby tail functioned in a more practical way, as well. Its bold black-and-white pattern was more than ornamental. Its dazzling white underside stood out in sharp contrast to its black-barred dorsal surface. When raised, this conspicuous tail patch was highly visible and, like a beacon, could be seen and followed even through dense underbrush. The mother bobcat held the tip of her tail erect and even waggled it like a beckoning finger when leading her young through heavy vegetation.

The bobcat's tufted ears were as elegantly decorative as was her tail, a matching pair of bright black and white accessories to set off her muted coat. A large white spot on the back of each one gave the cat the appearance of having rearview eyes. And by rotating these "ear-eyes" forward, a bobcat could produce the intimidating effect of being four-eyed.

Already the babies could flatten and twist their stiffening ears, and they did so as they tussled and spat and challenged one another in endless bouts of play. Their behavior closely paralleled that of domestic kittens of the same age, although some differences existed. For example, had a human being attempted to approach these wildcats, the infant felines would have responded with surprising ferocity. From the day their eyes had opened, they had possessed a warriorlike identification with their own wild natures.

Yet had they been encountered while still blind, they would have been tractable, might even have exhibited those traits of dependency and trust that so endear domestic kittens to their keepers. But in due course, even a bottle-reared bobcat would outgrow its early docility. Destined to become a peerless hunter, at maturity the animal would reject domesticity.

To prepare them for eventual independence, the mother bobcat did not always treat her kittens gently. When their antics exceeded what she could tolerate, she did not hesitate to snarl or cuff them with a loose paw. In actual fact, however, her blows carried little force. Unbalancing a kitten was all that was required to startle it into docility.

Nature had placed harsh demands on the female bobcat. Without help from a mate, she alone bore the burden of raising the young, of perpetuating the species, and now that her two kittens' developing senses gave them mobility, her task became exceedingly difficult.

Once the babies had explored the recesses of their cave home, they were eager to investigate the world outside. Like fledgling birds rocking on the edge of a nest, they teetered before the precipitous drop-off at their cave door. Below, in the dense willows, they could see the birds and animals that came to drink at the stream, and from above, they picked up a whiff of their mother's ascent trail, which led to the top of the cliff. But the kittens were as yet incapable of negotiating the widely spaced footholds. Their confinement in the cave, therefore, was temporarily ordained.

One day the female brought a kill back to the den. The still-warm body of the rabbit intrigued the kittens. The male took a swipe at its floppy ears while his mother plucked its fur. An incision

along its back released pooled blood, which the adult cat savored with closed eyes. She discarded the cecum before devouring the internal organs, then she ate her way into the rib cage. When a too-large segment of bone was swallowed, she coughed it up and reingested it. In short order, all edible parts disappeared. Only the skull, four hard feet, and the animal's cottony tail remained. These were appropriated by the kittens and became their first toys.

Within a few days' time, skulls and paws began to litter the cave floor and the infant kittens were joining their mother as she dined on kills. Gnawing meat relieved their sore gums, hard with emerging teeth. Tiny white points were surfacing and defining the little bobcats' carnivorous destiny. Absent from their mouths were the flat grinders typical of hoofed animals. For, unlike herbivores, the kittens would not need to pulverize large quantities of vegetable matter. On the contrary, their teeth were elegantly sharp weaponry designed to execute a fatal stab, to rip open hide, to crack bone. More than any other feature, it was the structure of these teeth that predestined the little cats to lead the life of hunters, with all that such a life entailed—irregular meals, vulnerability to rabbit cycles, and starvation, should injury or illness impair their ability to catch prey. Only by maintaining themselves at peak fitness would these young animals survive. For the bobcats' foreordained niche in the ecological system was the most demanding of all. In contrast to grazing animals, who are born on the bed of grass that later will feed them, the baby meat eaters had to learn quickly how to stalk and kill food.

Such skill as the kittens would have to acquire could best be learned through a long apprenticeship to their mother. For nine or ten months they would follow her about, learn where different kinds of prey might be found, observe her actions. Thus they would be provided with daily opportunities to practice their innate responses to prey, and throughout this period, their mother would supplement their sporadic catches with food contributions. Without her help, the kittens would certainly starve.

Not every mother animal that lived on the sage desert had to exert so much effort on behalf of her young. Most was demanded of the carnivores, those species that had to kill in order to eat. The female bobcat's behavior, had it been observed in a human being, would likely be called "selfless devotion." She, of course, did not measure her actions against any value system. Without knowledge of good or evil, she simply responded to her babies' needs. So long as rabbits were plentiful, she would provide her kittens with what surplus she could catch. This behavior was etched in DNA in her cells as indelibly as the tooth marks she carved on the bones that now were beginning to litter her cave.

That growing heap of rubble, mainly tails and feet of rabbits, was becoming an annoyance to the fastidious bobcat mother. Insects, attracted by the decaying waste, had begun to invade the cave. Prompted perhaps by her distaste for an untidy environment, she acted. In daring leaps, she carried her kittens, one by one, up the escarpment. No Flying Wallenda, handicapped by the weight of another body, ever executed more precise moves. A switchback in the route forced the bobcat to pirouette on a rock pinnacle, even as a limp kitten dangled precariously from her jaw.

Though the factor that triggered the mother bobcat's abrupt departure from her den very likely was its unsanitary condition, the time was precisely right for her kittens to become exposed to a wider world.

Chapter 4

The outside world did not frighten the kittens. Their round eyes fixed on every new sight with unwavering attention. Movement in particular attracted them. When something captured their interest, their pupils grew large, even changed shape. This reflex not only admitted more light onto their retinas, but enabled them to judge distances more accurately and better calculate the length leap needed to pounce on a desired object.

If the mother cat had moved the kittens earlier, before their vision was so well developed, the babies would have had difficulty navigating across unfamiliar terrain. Away from their natal den they lacked their own body-scent trails to guide them. Now, however, the young bobcats were visually ready to explore an unfamiliar environment, and their continued development required that they be exposed to an onslaught of new experiences. Soon they would have to begin to contribute to their own support, and even such patterns of predatory behavior as were instinctive in the little felines could only be performed well with practice.

The mother bobcat provided her babies with a role model. By imitating her actions, they could learn such things as how to wield a death bite to the small game they instinctively toyed with. For though stalking behavior came automatically to them, killing did not. Furthermore, in order to become skilled hunters, the babies would have to learn to put their instinctive impulses into an effective sequence. To do this, much practice was necessary.

Trailing behavior did not have to be learned. The babies kept their mother's tipped-up tail in sight and moved in her wake like a lineup of baby ducks. And, like ducklings, they waggled their own tail stumps as they wended their way through the sagebrush.

The trio headed west, moving toward the natal den in which the mother bobcat had delivered the firstborn male kitten. She was a creature of place, so much so that even the memory of intruders at that fateful location did not now dissuade her from returning. Within her home range, she made repeated use of a number of favorite resting ledges and dens, returning to them cyclically. A coyote mother would not have brought her young back to the scene of former trouble. But the bobcat's attachment to special haunts was powerful. For this reason the species was particularly vulnerable to trapping.

A wake of complaint followed the cats as they moved through the desert vegetation. Birds, sensitive to the presence of carnivores, chattered noisily as they passed. A startled ground sparrow cut short its burble of song in midphrase to sound a raucous alarm cry. Only a red-tailed hawk, riding on an updraft, tilted and looked down on the feline parade with an air of indifference.

When they arrived at the rock pile, the female bobcat did not immediately lead her kittens into the crevice which, for the next few weeks, would serve as their shelter. Instead, she climbed atop a gray boulder and stretched out. Warmed by the sun, the stone retained heat even though the late-afternoon air was beginning to cool. The kittens, after several attempts, managed to scale the rock also, and they joined their mother. All three cats, tired from the long trek, twined together and slept.

When they awoke, the setting sun had ignited the western sky, set it ablaze with shades of orange and crimson. The kittens crawled under their mother's body and began to nurse. With clasping forepaws they kneaded her breasts as they sucked the rich nutrients from her body. After they had finished, the mother cat stood up, produced a tongue-curling yawn, and leaped to the floor of the desert. Suddenly, she froze in her tracks. She had spotted a rabbit.

Down she sank into a crouch. She was in a state of high arousal now. An image had registered on her brain that caused her pupils to widen, sent adrenaline coursing through her body. Her actions could not now be restrained; they could only be reordered according to the signals and movements produced by the prey before her.

With eyes fixated on her target, she slid forward, her body held low, her ears flattened, each paw meeting the ground as soundlessly as a settling feather. Like an insidious shadow, she moved, pausing frequently. She was endowed both with a capacity to hold abso-

lutely still when necessary, no matter how awkward the stance she must maintain, and with the capacity to wait interminable stretches of time, sustained by her tension. Her eyes never shifted away from the terror-stricken rabbit.

The rabbit was not so self-controlled. It raised its head, and, at that instant, in an explosion of movement, the cat made her rush. Swiftly, she pinned her victim under her chest and, bracing for a struggle, dug her hind claws into the ground. Scanning the rabbit's neck with her mouth, she quickly located the vital spot to bite. The rabbit screamed, and its cry released the cat's power to kill. Her fangs pried their way between two neck vertebrae and wedged them apart, snapping the rabbit's spinal cord. Afterward, no marks were visible where the two bloodless puncture wounds had been made.

Life at the rock pile offered the kittens a variety of learning experiences. Inside their den, they raced about through a maze of spaces they discovered in between the big stones. Outside, they scampered about after insects and played hide-and-seek in the sage. When they tired, they climbed atop boulders and sunned themselves.

The kittens were masterfully camouflaged. As they lay draped on the pocked rocks, their spotted coats appeared to merge with the backdrop. Even their plump bodies seemed to mimic the lumpy shapes of stones. At rest, they were so difficult to distinguish that birds would sometimes land within striking range of them. On such occasions, the kittens would take a flying leap at the fluttery creatures, but they were not yet quick enough to seize one.

Every moving object, every rustling sound brought the young bobcats into a state of high alert, tuned up their nervous systems. Stalking, hiding, pouncing—these activities were innate to the whole of the family Felidae: lions, ocelots, jaguars, domestic cats—all performed these instinctive movements. The bobcat kittens practiced these predatory moves on one another with no harmful results. Their bites were inhibited. Their raking swipes were made with partially retracted claws and directed, for the most part, at one another's shoulders and necks, areas thick with hair. They frequently reversed roles. Sometimes one kitten would wrestle the other to the ground, forepaws locked around "victim's" neck. Then the vanquished kitten would gain the upper hand and bring down its attacker.

Still, they did not know how to kill. When the female cat brought them a live baby kangaroo rat, they chased and worried it, but made no attempt to execute the fatal bite. Like a human child with a windup toy, their excitement mounted whenever the creature suddenly reversed direction or moved swiftly away. But when their play object halted, they prodded it with a soft paw to make it go again. Their only objective was to dart after the terrorized creature. Eventually, the kangaroo rat made its escape, scurrying into a small hole in the ground. For a long time the kittens kept watch outside the burrow, but the rodent did not emerge, and in time they forgot about it.

When the moon was full their mother took them on their first night prowl. They traveled a fair distance from the rock pile, strolling along the periphery of the female cat's home range. From time

to time she stopped, backed up to a shrub or rock, and sprayed it with a drop of strong-smelling urine. With the passage of time, such scent postings lost their message content. Only by frequently spraying her regular travel routes could the female keep visiting bobcats advised of her mood and her continued presence in the place. To underscore the message, she sometimes scraped the ground beside a scent station. In the event that wind dissipated the odor she deposited, these visible grooves, carved in the dirt, would also serve as notice of her passage.

Now the female made an exploratory junket, traveling a short distance onto a neighbor cat's customary range. There a pile of fresh, unburied stools prompted her to make an unhurried retreat. The scat informed her that the resident cat was female, a mother, and making current use of the area. The place, therefore, held no further attraction for the intruding female bobcat.

The bobcat's tendency to avoid its own kind served the species well. As a result, animals spaced themselves widely and, in so doing, inadvertently prevented prey populations from becoming overexploited. Avoidance behavior also guaranteed each cat an adequate number of den sites and hiding places. Depending upon the quality of the terrain, a female bobcat in the Idaho desert might require an area of from five to twenty square miles to support herself and her kittens. Within this range, she frequently moved about, bivouacking at various den sites at different times of the year. Thus she allowed pockets of rabbits time to breed and recover from her own hunting pressure before once again preying on them. Rest-and-rotation was not a concept dreamed up by human agriculturists.

Rabbits and hares were the bobcat's mainstay. The white-tailed jackrabbit—actually a hare—provided the greatest quantity of meat, but it was more difficult to ambush than were the true rabbits. More often than not, the bobcat left these hares for the coyotes to course after, and she preyed instead upon cottontails and pygmy rabbits. Less important prey species were the grouse, kangaroo rats, weasels, mice, pack rats, and lizards, which added variety to the mother bobcat's diet. But rabbits and hares, animals of the order Lagomorpha, constituted the major part of her diet. Without a good supply of these creatures, she stood little chance of raising a litter of kittens.

In part because of her dependency on rabbits, the bobcat spent much of the day resting and hunted during the evening hours when

cottontails became active. This perhaps explained why her species had evolved such excellent nighttime vision. Whereas her daytime pupils were elliptical, after dark they grew round and expanded almost to fill her entire eye socket. In addition, at the back of each eye, a reflective membrane called a tapetum gathered stray light and enhanced her vision.

The bobcat was elegantly designed to play her part in the scheme of things. And in the scheme of things, her fate and the fate of rabbits and hares were inextricably intertwined. Predator and prey alike depended on one another for their long-term well-being. The rabbit served to feed the cat; the cat's role was to weed the rabbit, to suppress its population. The balance that existed between these animals was a dynamic one. When rabbit crashes occurred, as they normally did on a cyclical basis, it was the rabbit that regulated the bobcat population, for without that important food item, bobcats had a difficult time raising their young.

Just such a situation prevailed in the Idaho desert now, and had done so for more than five years. The rabbit populations had been unusually slow in recovering from a low that should not have lasted half that time. As a result, during the whole of this period, the female bobcat had failed to raise a single kitten born to her. Now, once again, she was about to be put to the test. The food demands of her new babies were beginning to escalate, and, though she was experiencing a corresponding impulse to hunt more frequently, she had to travel ever farther afield to locate prey. And the greater the distance she ranged, the more energy she consumed, with the result that she herself often ate what rabbits she finally killed and brought nothing back to her offspring.

One fact of bobcat life was elemental, unequivocal: while her kittens were young, the mother bobcat needed to make a living close to home. But lacking a handy supply of rabbits, she would have great difficulty keeping both herself and her young alive. In such circumstances, she would eventually opt for her own survival and allow her kittens to perish. Nature most values an animal of breeding status.

Chapter 5

To the casual observer, the silver and dust-green sagebrush plain that the bobcat family inhabited appeared flat and empty of life. But it was full of surprises. The great sweep of desert was as undulant as the sea. Its gentle swells and troughs concealed rock craters, lost rivers banked with cottonwoods, and volcanic lava flows upon whose ancient crusts clung twisted junipers. These points of relief were significant places to the animals of the Idaho desert. The female bobcat visited, marked, and utilized many such features that occurred within her range.

Rimming this expanse of desert were towering mountain chains whose lower slopes, moraines, and draws dropped gently into sagebrush country and offered entry to the lush world above. But the foothills were deceptive. Access to the lofty places—the wet meadows and fragrant conifer forests—was, in fact, restricted to those surefooted animals capable of clinging to mountainsides too steep and windy to hold ground cover. Bobcats, of course, could move with ease between the two worlds.

Yet individual bobcats were often limited to either desert or mountain clime by the behavioral barricades of their neighbors. The female bobcat occupied mainly desert floor, and only a few acres of foothill fell within her home range. Except during mating season, she made little contact with the male cat who inhabited the mountain terrain above her. Though their territories were adjacent, his scent marks contained her inside her own hunting ground like some magic circle drawn around a devil-worshipping tribesman.

As a result, his way of life and hers differed. The female cat was adapted to desert prey. When rabbits were scarce, she snared other small prey and did not bother the antelope that herded on the flat from November through March. Nor did she attack the black-tailed deer that browsed along the streambed. By contrast, the male bobcat sometimes needed to feed on larger animals in order to build up sufficient reserves to winter in the mountains. Though he, too, favored a lagomorph diet—in particular, the varying hare—he also occasionally jumped a deer. And a seventy-five-pound beaver equipped with three-inch teeth was not beyond the reach of his ambition. Considering that he carried only half that weight on his own lithe frame, this feat was all the more remarkable.

Both cats had been taught to exploit their respective environments by their mothers, who, by virtue of having themselves survived the vicissitudes of mountain or desert life, were well qualified to be role models. Each had raised young who, when grown, sought conditions in which to locate that were most familiar to them. Thus the high born male made his home in the mountains and preyed on animals his mother had also hunted; by the same token, the female bobcat looked for a desert niche to occupy.

Such behavioral versatility had served the North American bobcat well. Over its four-million-year history, twelve subspecies had evolved, each geared to a different environment. Hair length and color, skull size and shape, even the prominence of ear tufts distinguished one subspecies from another and reflected the biotic community that had produced the type. Even within a particular population, individual bobcats expressed this protean capacity. Not all cats looked or acted alike.

It was not so remarkable, therefore, that the male bobcat, in response to harsh winters, was a much larger animal than his desert brothers. Nor was it strange that his rufous-tinged coat had grown long and thick, like the pelt of a Canada lynx. In fact, he closely resembled that species of cat, for his muttonchops were exceptionally wide, and his ears were topped by tufts that stood over an inch tall, like a pair of feathers in an Indian headband. From any distance, he might easily have been mistaken for a lynx, though upon close inspection it became apparent that he lacked the furry snowshoe paws that could support that animal atop deep drifts.

In spring, nature's demands on his climate-shaped body were minimal. Unlike his mate, he was not encumbered with family responsibilities. While she labored to provide their offspring with food, he enjoyed a season of leisure. His lack of participation in family life was less a matter of indifference on his part than intolerance on hers. Any chance encounter between himself and the kittens along the border of their contiguous habitats inevitably resulted in conflict. No matter how placid a demeanor he presented, the mother cat routed him.

For his part, the mountain male was an exceptionally mild-mannered individual and rarely exhibited hostile behavior toward other members of his species, even during mating season. It was unlikely, therefore, that he would have destroyed newborn kittens—behavior often attributed to male bobcats. That he would have harmed young already strong enough to accompany their mother was even less probable. On the contrary, given his temperament, he might have assisted in their education! But the mother bobcat's antagonism toward others at this time did not allow for such a social experiment to take place. Like females from time immemorial, she labored, unassisted, to feed and protect her young. And like father bobcats throughout the animal's long history, the male steered clear of trouble and avoided contact with the little family.

Abundance of prey in spring made it easy for the male cat to satisfy his needs, which were minimal during this mild season, and so he spent most of every day stretched out on a high rock shelf absorbing the warmth of the sun. At dusk, when the wingbeats of owls told him rabbits were becoming active, he would rouse himself, descend from his ledge, and secure one for dinner.

This was the season of molt. Like the varying hare he so relished, the male bobcat's thick winter fur was falling out in patches, giving him a piebald appearance. And again like the varying hare, he tried to hurry the shedding process along by vigorously licking his flanks, shoulders, sides, and back. He scrubbed hard-to-reach places, such as his dotted ears, with the inside of a well-moistened foreleg, his sheathed paws being poorly designed for such work.

When too much grooming resulted in the ingestion of hair balls, he sought the emetic properties of grass. A trip to the high meadow where it grew also relieved the monotony of his spring situation and, on occasion, even provided the languorous cat with an unexpected and beneficial adventure. Deprived of such diversion, he would likely have groomed himself raw, like a bored zoo cat.

One day a surfeit of sunning prompted him to plunge from his rock perch and head for higher slopes. He strode past an aspen grove where a female hare was raising a litter of seven. Though the wind was strong and carried on it the news of the young leverets,

the bobcat was not waylaid by this information. A wad of fur in his stomach was causing him discomfort, and he knew where to find grass to relieve the condition.

In an undeviating course, he padded uphill toward a familiar plateau. But as he drew near his destination, a more distracting message was wafted to his nostrils. The bobcat wrinkled his nose and drew up his lip in a grimace. He was not expressing revulsion. On the contrary, the bobcat was savoring scent, or flehming. With rapid flicks of his tongue, he lapped in the provocative odor, directing it upward to the ducts that led to his Jacobson's organ, an auxiliary "nose" with which he analyzed smells of particular interest.

A heady sensation flowed through his body. The pasture contained a type of wild thyme whose effect on his brain was no less pleasurable than was catnip. Chirping like a bird, he sprinted onto the coarse weeds and began to roll, rubbing his body across the aromatic plants again and again until the patch was reduced to stubble. Then, ecstatically, he lay face up, chortling and inhaling the intoxicating odors released by the crushed vegetation. The hairball in his stomach was forgotten; the ennui that had prompted him to set out on this junket was forgotten. With half-closed eyes he rocked

and rolled and lay upturned, the long white hairs of his belly gleaming in the sunlight.

A spotted fawn rose to its feet and peered at the spectacle. But the bobcat took no notice of the curious youngster whose mother had left it alone while she went off to browse in an aspen stand. The doe was not neglectful of her baby. It was appropriate that the young fawn spend most of every day by itself while its more visible mother visited her favorite feeding places. The infant deer was not yet fleet enough to make a swift escape, and, for its own protection, the doe sequestered it in the small range she had staked out just for that purpose, an area she defended from all other deer.

The white-tailed fawn was beautifully camouflaged. Dapples across its back broke up the image of its total form and mimicked the kaleidoscope of sunlight that played on the grassy meadow. When alarmed, the fawn instinctively dropped to the ground and remained as motionless as lichen-splotched rock.

But today the little deer's fright response was not aroused by the sight of an erratically behaving bobcat rolling in a patch of weeds. Perhaps even at so tender an age, the fawn was capable of reading the mood of a predatory animal. And this predator was not sending signals of aggressive intent, did not even appear to notice the fawn. Wallowing in the aromatic herb, the male bobcat acted in a manner strangely reminiscent of a sexually aroused female cat. Indeed, he may well have been experiencing something like female eroticism, for the cells in his hypothalamus, which were excited by the odor of thyme, were the same cells that, in a female cat, are sensitive to her own sex hormones.

The fawn craned its neck and tested the scent-laden air with its wet nose. The pungent odor that created such euphoria in the bobcat produced no effect whatsoever on the deer's hypothalamus. What motivated its moves was ordinary curiosity. Tentatively, with one foreleg raised in readiness to flee, it leaned down and touched the pink, upside-down nose of the rolling cat with its own black one. Then, suddenly, perhaps startled by its own audacity, it sprang backward and began racing about the field.

By now the bobcat was beginning to come out of his trancelike state, and the sight of the bounding fawn attracted his attention. Quickly, he righted himself and, with wide eyes, began tracking the movements of the high-spirited young herbivore.

So long as the fawn capered about erratically, it was in no immediate danger of being attacked. The bobcat was no courser and preferred not to pursue unpredictable quarry. The bobcat was a careful and efficient hunter, would sometimes even desist from making an attack if an animal seemed cognizant of his presence. Yet he was capable of vanquishing the most formidable prey and cleverly employed a variety of hunting strategies. He even knew how to lay a trap for his victims. Near some place of concealment, he would drop scraps of food, and, when some hungry animal came to his bait, he would ambush it from the cover.

Now he feigned lack of interest in the fawn and began to groom himself in what seemed to be an attempt to lull it into a false sense of security. Rhythmically, he dragged his rough tongue down one shoulder and across his back, while, with each lift of his head, he took careful note of the leaping fawn's whereabouts. He had perfect knowledge of his own prowess. He knew the length of his longest leap, and now he waited for his victim to move within this fatal distance. At that instant he would sail onto its back and fasten his jaws and claws around its slim neck.

When catching smaller prey, the bobcat sometimes tossed and played with a captive, even allowing it a few near escapes before he would kill it. Large animals, however, he did not toy with. From watching his mother, the bobcat had learned how to ambush a fully grown deer. He did so only after it had bedded down. Then he would make a sudden pounce onto the withers of the unsuspecting victim and hang on with tooth and claw while the frenzied animal dashed about trying to shake off its grim rider.

His first such wild ride had been exhilarating, and when it had culminated in the death of the deer, he had been somewhat surprised. That attack had been initiated, not out of hunger, nor from any desire to kill; the attack had been launched merely to give vent to the cat's neurological readiness to stalk and pounce on something. Far less frequently, other neural assemblages in his brain built up an appetite to inflict a killing bite. But his predatory impulses were not always in synchrony. Nevertheless, he afterward connected the benefit obtained—a large quantity of meat—with the sight of live deer. And in winter, when hunger impelled him, he headed for a snowy swale where a herd of does yarded. Had it not been for this food source, he would have had great difficulty surviving seven long months of polar weather in the high country. For in winter many prey species hibernated or lived so deep beneath the snow pack that they were beyond the reach of a hungry bobcat.

At the same time, bringing down an animal eight times his weight was a dangerous business, and he did not undertake it carelessly. Success was infrequent and depended on the element of surprise. Healthy adult deer seldom failed to note his lurking presence. Injured, malnourished, or sick individuals were less attentive and more frequently fell victim to him, but even these animals, once provoked, could run down a bobcat and trample him to death. The mountain bobcat launched all his attacks on deer where nearby trees or rock crevices could provide instant sanctuary.

In spring, when rodents and rabbits were plentiful, it was not necessary for a bobcat to take such a risk. On the other hand, in spring the birth of vulnerable fawns revived his interest in venison. Any untended baby deer, although difficult to discover, was easy to kill. And on this day, fate seemed to be delivering a meal to him.

While the fawn tired itself out bounding about the meadow, the bobcat waited. Patience was natural to the cat. Lying in wait was a habit he indulged in even when there was little likelihood that prey would pass his way. At the same time, the moment the young deer dropped to the ground, he was swift to act.

Through the tall vegetation he crept, his belly so low to the ground that his elbows bowed, his rubbery paw pads riding soundlessly over every pebble and stick. Stealthily, eyes fixed on his target, he slid, his movements all coordinated grace, his energy fluid and streaming through unresisting muscles. Only the quivering tip of his abbreviated tail betrayed the great tension he was now experiencing.

The fawn's big ears pricked up and swished like fans. The youngster sensed danger, and adrenaline pumped through its bloodstream, energizing it for flight. At the same time a signal from its brainstem gave a conflicting order to freeze.

The cat stopped behind a chokecherry bush and took stock of his silent progress. A slink-run to a fieldstone would now close the last piece of ground between himself and his victim. This was the critical move. If the fawn did not now catch sight of him and bolt to safety, the cat would be in position to attack. From the fieldstone, in a single stretch-lunge, he could leap upon the baby deer and, with his grappling-hook foreclaws, grasp its withers and pull it onto its side. The ensuing struggle would last only so long as it took the cat's mouth to find the fawn's neck.

The fawn could not see the cat whose scent it had picked up, and, in an effort to locate this threat, it swiveled its head. This movement served the bobcat, helped him to maintain a precise bearing on his victim.

The mountain bobcat was in perfect form. Hunting was a tonic to him, essential to his well-being. Without this outlet for his accumulated energies, a bobcat could fall victim to neurological disturbances, might even begin to misjudge distances and bump into things. Hunting provided more than food for his stomach. Hunting nourished a bobcat's nervous system.

Now, streaking full tilt toward the fieldstone, the mountain bobcat was fulfilling his destiny, satisfying a physical need and performing an important role in the food chain. He did not see the doe come bounding from behind. He did not see the rage in her face, her flaring nostrils and gaping mouth. One crack on his spine extinguished his life. In a moment, all memory, all experience, all emotion, all awareness, all competence, all intelligence dissolved into absolute nothingness.

With daggerlike hoofs, the doe continued to pummel the bobcat long after his body had been reduced to a ragged pelt. Again and again she stomped, until the rush of energy that had launched her, arrow-swift, across the field was at last dissipated. When she was done, she went in search of her fawn, who had bounded off and now lay as inert as a stone in the long shadow of a ponderosa pine.

For some time the doe's repeated calls failed to release her baby from its functional paralysis. Finally, however, the urgency of her bleats stirred something in its young memory. Lifting its dished face, the little creature mewled. The doe's ears cupped. She took a fix on the sound and quickly located her offspring. After the two had greeted, she licked it all over.

For many decades the skeletal remains of the mountain bobcat would lie concealed in tall grasses whose nourishment would be taken from the cat's decayed body. Sometimes rabbits would come to feed on this enriched vegetation. And, fittingly, offspring of these rabbits would someday become food for bobcats. So biomass would flow through the wild community, uninterrupted, powering life, finding form and expression in plants and animals high and low on the food chain, a theater-in-the-round with a revolving cast of characters and a single theme. In nature no life is wasted.

SUMMER

Chapter 6

Rabbits were not coming back. Six years had passed since the lagomorph population had peaked, triggering an inevitable crash the following year. By now numbers should have been on the upswing again, but something had happened. The eleven-year boom-and-bust rabbit cycle had gone out of phase and wildlife managers were at a loss to explain why. For, despite the fact that they were charged with the responsibility of managing Idaho's wildlife, nature, in fact, was performing the job—and in her own mysterious way.

Not that game managers were much concerned over the matter. Rabbits were not an important "target animal," like deer or grouse, whose population fluctuations directly affected the amount of revenue collected by the Idaho Department of Fish and Game. It was not necessary to purchase a hunting license to shoot a rabbit.

By contrast, had one of the horned or antlered species suffered such a setback, the department would have had to answer for the decline to irate hunters, whose license fees financed their operation. Thus, the department was bent on promoting ever greater numbers of elk, deer, antelope, and bighorn sheep. And often the strategies they employed to achieve this end had adverse affects on "non-target species."

In some instances, predatory animals that fed on target species were deliberately killed off. At other times, the animal that was eliminated was not a predator, but merely competed with a desired game animal for food. The interdependency of all life in each and every ecosystem was either poorly understood or simply ignored by the public servants whose job it was to look after the state's wildlife.

And this policy of "single-species management" was not unique to Idaho.

Rabbits, so important a food to owls, foxes, coyotes, bobcats, hawks, and eagles, were granted no protection. A rabbit could be shot any day of the year and by boys too young to qualify for a license to hunt other game. But it was not ten-year-old boys who were the rabbits' real enemy. Rabbits consumed grass, lettuce—all kinds of vegetable crops. Whenever rabbits became numerous, a group of Idaho growers undertook to effect their mass destruction. "Rabbit beats" were held in which entire families participated. Droves of people would fan out and move across the land, spooking every rabbit from cover. Children earned high praise for clubbing panicked animals to death.

What impact this organized carnage had on owls, hawks, coyotes, and bobcats, whose populations were tied to rabbit fluctuations, did not seem to concern these particular growers. They felt no more compassion for predators than they did for the rabbits they slaughtered. Wild predators were sometimes "guilty" of killing their stock, so these animals, too, had to be destroyed. Public wildlife on public lands was poisoned, trapped, gassed, and burned—and often at taxpayers' expense. State and federal agencies were heavily committed to their "predator control" programs, and millions of public dollars were spent to eradicate hundreds of thousands of badgers, coyotes, bobcats, hawks, bear, and mountain lions that lived on the public lands.

It was not altogether surprising, therefore, that the rabbit cycle was out of synchrony. The normal adjusting mechanisms that, in a wild community, act on numbers of plant and animal species to compensate for over- or underproduction were constantly being upset. One result was hardship for the female bobcat.

Her kittens were growing rapidly, and each day demanded larger quantities of solid food. To locate scarce cottontails or jackrabbits, she ranged ever farther from her den site. But more often than not, she brought nothing back to her young.

Now they were making other demands on her, too. It was time for them to learn to kill, and each day the mother bobcat brought them a live mouse to play with. The female kitten showed more aptitude for chasing and pouncing on these offerings than did her brother and one day even made a determined attempt to kill one. But the mouse she nipped was more than a match for her. Taking a

50

defensive stance, the feisty creature stood on its hind legs and, turning round and round, eyeballed her and squeaked until the baby bobcat grew so disconcerted she withdrew to the rock pile. The mouse escaped unharmed.

That the voles and white-footed mice the mother bobcat presented to her kittens were in such lively, fighting form was no accident. She carried the luckless creatures in a soft mouth to cause them no injury. In a few months time, her kittens would live or die by their hunting proficiency, and a half-dead training mouse would not prepare them for this harsh eventuality. Only by toying with highly responsive prey could they learn to judge pounce distances and anticipate sudden moves.

Although the mother bobcat supervised her kittens' daily skirmishes with live bait, she did not join in their sport. Only when a mouse threatened to escape would she rouse herself, recapture the harassed creature, and deliver it once again to her young. Eventually, after they had enjoyed perhaps an hour of this, she might suddenly snuff out the life of their tormented victim. Then, in an insistent voice, she would call her kittens to come and eat it.

Rats were a different story. These animals she did not bring to her young. Even a chance encounter with one of the big pack rats that inhabited the desert brought out the assassin in her. If she spied one wandering about the sage, it stood little chance of reaching the safety of its big stick house. Hungry or not, the bobcat would kill it on sight and afterward prevent her kittens from approaching its carcass. She seemed to be aware of a rat's ability to overpower a young kitten.

The kittens were now almost ten weeks old, a critical period in their lives. It was at this age that they spontaneously began performing certain predatory moves. Should their "hunting lessons" be postponed, their aptitude for killing prey would begin to wane. If delayed too long, certain lessons might never be learned, for like human infants who at a particular stage show readiness to walk or talk, the baby bobcats at ten weeks were experiencing a learning peak.

In one sense, the kittens already knew every move required to bring down prey. Pouncing, lying in wait, chasing, stalking, tossing, jumping—even the nape bite—were present in working order in their central nervous systems. However, assembling these disparate actions into purposeful sequences and manifesting such behavior in

appropriate circumstances required learning. Also, certain moves could only be performed when the kittens were in a state of high excitement; as yet, the young bobcats were incapable of intentional behavior.

It was not at all strange that, day after day, the kittens chased and pounced and tossed their practice mice and yet failed to inflict a killing bite. Different levels of arousal elicited different kinds of activity. And to release the kill bite, extreme excitement was required. Thus nature had protected the kittens from making casual use of the lethal fangs and claws with which they were equipped. If killing behavior had been as easily evoked as was stalking or pouncing, the baby bobcats would likely have inflicted mortal wounds on one another in early bouts of play.

On the other hand, not much stimulation was needed to incite them to sneak up on leaves or to scurry after strange noises. They frequently performed these harmless maneuvers, also important to their ultimate survival. By contrast to the killing bite, interest in this activity had to be easily and frequently aroused, for a bobcat, by necessity, would have to stalk many more animals than it would ultimately catch and kill. It could not grow tired of repeating this maneuver, however many times it ended in failure.

So it was that the kittens were slow to learn that their toys were meant to be killed and eaten. Even after their mother would convert one into a carcass, she would have to "tell" her kittens it was now food. They watched, round-eyed, as time after time she demonstrated just how the act of execution should be performed. Often, afterward, they would resume tossing the defunct mouse and have to be reminded to eat.

This "relief play" was also necessary behavior. It dissipated the excitement and fear that mounted in them while stalking and pouncing on live prey. One day this excitement would override a certain threshold, reaching a killing pitch. Then their most difficult lesson would be learned, their ultimate predatory response would be acquired.

Meanwhile, their mother provided all their meals. She made different sounds when she presented them with different species of prey. A fairly mild tone announced that a mouse was now dead and edible. When she returned from a hunt with a dead rat in her jaws, the intensity of her call told them that what she carried had recently been dangerous. The kittens seemed to grasp her message and

would approach cautiously. Her sound for "rabbit" was a satisfied chortle. Unfortunately, they seldom heard that news.

One day the diligent mother cat brought them prey that was rabbit-sized but covered with feathers—a sage grouse. In so doing, she seemed to be exhibiting ingenuity, for her growing kittens could no longer subsist on a ration of tiny mice. For the next two weeks, grouse became the bobcats' mainstay.

This prey, which did not behave like earthbound rabbits, required of the bobcat a quite different predatory tactic. Though this ground bird was not as difficult to catch as were birds that could take off swiftly and make a rapid ascent, it nevertheless presented a challenge. An aerial escape route was one the bobcat could not follow, and a grouse, after a labored lift-off, soon gained sufficient momentum to soar beyond her reach.

The bobcat dropped the "slow stalk" from her attack strategy and instead made an instant leap upon every so-called fool hen she saw before it gathered wit to fly. But because evolution had preadapted her to hunt ground prey, to hold fast to the earth with her hind claws while dispatching a victim, her performance at snatching birds out of the air was sometimes awkward. On occasion, when she lost contact with the ground, she would catapult into a somersault. After such a misfire, she spent much time grooming herself, while she recovered her aplomb. At best, she was a mediocre hunter of sage grouse.

Nevertheless, the birds she did catch were good-sized, almost as large as wild turkeys, and they provided adequate food for her family. Dragging such a prize to her den, however, was cumbersome work. Sometimes the mother bobcat ate a portion of her victim before attempting to move it. Then again, her efforts to reduce the bird's size would fail to alter its weight. For by biting twenty feathers off the creature's long tail, she could not significantly lighten her load.

At first her kittens showed little enthusiasm for the sagey-tasting fowl. But a number of rabbitless days convinced them to eat whatever their mother brought. In the end, they developed an appetite for the bird, even helped strip offerings of their feathers, a job they performed less punctiliously than did one of their relatives, the fastidious mountain lion.

But sage grouse did not offer a lasting solution to the bobcats' food problem. Numbers were limited. Unlike the prolific rabbit family, grouse did not reproduce on a monthly basis; a sage hen hatched only a single brood of chicks each year, and soon no more birds could be located by the assiduous bobcat. Once again the family suffered hunger.

One day the female bobcat decided to move her family. The impulse came upon her quite suddenly. It was not a logical decision based on an intelligent assessment of available food resources in the area. She was incapable of applying such human reason to her problem of want. Yet her subjective experience of hunger created a restless urge in her to look elsewhere for food.

The kittens were informed of their imminent departure by their mother's pacing and the nervous twitching of her tail, which seemed to be discharging energy like some kind of lightning rod. When she called to them they were ready to be off. Holding their own stubby tails erect, they fell into line behind her.

Chapter 7

The bobcats returned to the stream. This time, however, the mother cat did not take possession of her former den high on the cliff face. Instead, she led her kittens down a steep deer trail to the canyon bottom, where, during the cats' absence, rushes and willows had grown up along the stream bank. It was an ideal place for them, rife with small animals such as chipmunks and voles; yet the dense underbrush presented a barrier to any bear or mountain lion who might come to drink at the stream.

Upon their arrival, the kittens set about exploring their new surroundings. The closely set willow stems created a maze of runways, an ideal arena for playing hide-and-seek. The male kitten responded to his new environment with a display of high spirits; he sprinted off into the thicket, out of sight of his mother and sister. After a short time, however, when neither came looking for him, his exuberant mood changed to one of anxiety, clearly discernible in the birdlike S.O.S. signals he began to send out.

The kittens rarely produced the mewing sounds typical of ordinary house cats. Nevertheless, their vocal repertoire was by no means limited. Chirps, chortles, screams, huffs, hisses, growls, purrs, and even barks enabled them to express what mood of the moment possessed them. Now, twittering like an alarmed wren, the distressed male kitten alerted his sister to his whereabouts, and, in no time, she located, stalked, and ambushed him. As the two rolled about on the dank-smelling earth, forepaws clasped about necks, they raked each other's vulnerable undersides with retracted hind claws. But despite the appearance of unrestrained violence their wild play conveyed, they inflicted no injuries on one another. When one of the kittens succeeded in extricating itself from what appeared

to be a deadly clasp, it would dash through brush, hide, and impatiently wait to be discovered again. At that delicious moment, the mock battle would resume.

For several hours following their arrival, the mother bobcat relaxed beside the fast-moving water and lazily watched her young at play. From time to time, as one or the other of them flew past her, she would topple and groom it. She also gave herself a thorough cleaning.

The temperature at the stream was ten degrees cooler than on the sage plain above, and this condition was what allowed the bobcat family to remain active. For now, in summer, the heat of the desert sun normally discouraged diurnal activity, holding the bobcats to cover until dusk. After a time, the female bobcat, accustomed to sleeping at this hour, grew weary, and she began to look for a cavity in the cliff in which to hole up.

Behind the bank of willows, the cliff jutted skyward as vertically as a citadel wall and extended for many miles up and down the stream. Its ancient face sheltered many animals. The age-old river that had carved a canyon here had, during its ever deepening course, eroded innumerable grottoes and recesses along its slowly lowering banks. Most of these niches, marks of past water levels, now stood high above the present-day stream. But it was not one of these lofty dwelling places that the bobcat now sought. Her kittens were too large to be toted up and down a steep precipice and were not yet sufficiently surefooted to maneuver the climb themselves. So the mother cat chose a deep, hollowed-out place at the base of the cliff, fronted by a tangle of vegetation that extended to the very edge of the stream. Inside, the cave was dry and contained no offensive pack-rat droppings. The female inspected cracks and crevices for snakes. Finding no sign of them, she curled up in a cool corner and dozed off.

That she was in no particular hurry to collect her young and lead them to this new place of shelter was not surprising. She needed a respite from their irrepressible playfulness and relentless demands. The rabbit shortage, compounded by the strain of nursing, had drained her energies. And her breasts were sore and scratched from her babies' claws and fully erupted baby teeth. A less devoted mother, suffering these painful consequences of nursing, might have weaned her ten-week-old kittens and forced them to exist on what solid food she could provide for them. But the mater-

nal bond between this female and her young was strong. When her kittens mobbed her for milk, she nearly always submitted. Only on rare occasions, noting their intentions in advance, would she quietly slip away and hide.

Now, curled up in her newly staked-out den, she slept soundly. And if the noise of her young thrashing about in brush figured in her dream state, the sounds did not disturb her rest. She knew this part of her range well. She felt no anxiety over the safety of her kittens here.

Nor did the kittens experience any insecurity over being left untended in a strange place. They had long ago become accustomed to their mother's periodic absences. Her rabbit hunts often kept her away from them for as long as twenty-four hours. Moreover, their new surroundings so intrigued them, they hardly even noticed their hunger pangs, despite the fact that two days had passed since they had ingested any solid food. Environmental stimulation was in itself a kind of food to the developing kittens. Every new experience they devoured with ravenous enthusiasm. Every waking hour they spent scatting after crickets or leaping at butterflies. And if reality

failed to provide the stimulation they craved, they attacked phantom prey. Now they raced about in the sticklike willows and burned energy, until, at last, their hunger could no longer be ignored. But the one who could remedy this condition was nowhere in sight. Both kittens began to call.

If their provider heard their cries, she did not make any response. Her earlier compulsion to keep her young under constant surveillance had waned. Now, as their wails grew more insistent, she merely lifted her head and listened. Then, as if satisfied that her offspring were remaining in the vicinity, she drifted back to sleep. When the kittens could raise no answering chirrup, they twined together like a pair of fuzzy gray and orange caterpillars and they, too, slept. An hour's rest refreshed them. When they awoke, they were ready to engage in more high jinks, and they played their way down to the edge of the stream. There, once again, they investigated the properties of water.

The sight of their own reflections at first aroused their curiosity, then their hostility. The more precocious female kitten was the first to go on the offensive. Lowering her big ears until their eyespots were visible from the front, she wrinkled up her face and hissed. The insult was instantly returned by her liquid reflection, and both littermates jumped backward in tandem. But as soon as their alarm had subsided, the pair crept back to the bank to have another look. There they found the two strange kittens had also returned and were peering up at them! Now the male acted. With a splayed paw, he swatted the water and dissolved his rival into ripples and bubbles. Then, after shaking the cold stuff from his foot, he strutted back and forth along the edge of the stream.

But his enemy soon rematerialized and did so wearing the same self-satisfied expression on his round face as that of the male kitten. The male kitten hunched his shoulders, and from his throat there rolled a tiny growl. Then, rearing on his hind legs, he sprang at this foe, who, of course, retaliated in kind. But the mocking cat in the water was insubstantial and could not repel the force on an oncoming attacker. Over the bank, the male kitten toppled. Down he sank into turbulent, cold water, while his startled sister jumped backward and looked on.

In seconds, the submerged kitten surfaced. Automatic swimming motions raised him, but his scrabbling strokes were ineffectual against the strong current, which sent him skimming downstream like a water bug. It carried him a hundred and fifty yards, then pinned him against a stone.

The kitten clutched at the rock's slippery sides and tried to raise himself again and again. At last he did succeed in clawing his way onto the stone's protruding surface, but the sanctuary was a precarious one. Water eddied and burbled around him. He was cold and drenched to his hide; his vision was blurred, his ears clogged. But no amount of discomfort could have induced him to release one paw from his four-footed grip on the rock that supported him—even to take a fast wipe at a wet eye or rub a wet ear. With the tenacity of a raptor whose claws have locked around prey, he clung. And the noise of the water rushing round him on all sides drowned out his distress calls.

Hours passed and the sky lost its hard brilliance. A few birds began to glide on the late-afternoon air currents. Dusk came to the shady gulch. Nocturnal birds, owls and nighthawks, left their sleeping perches in the cliff wall and began to swoop after rodents, even before diurnal birds on the still-bright plain above had finished singing their evening songs. Yet the kitten managed to hold on to the rock. His voice had long since given out; his claws, however, continued to opt for survival.

And at some distance upstream, the female kitten hid in the willow thicket. The abrupt departure of her sibling had created great anxiety in her, and for some time thereafter she had cleaned her fur. Whenever she was distressed, she would apply herself to this task. Now, however, this "displacement behavior" brought her no relief. She had never before been separated from her brother, and she did not like being alone. For, though she was destined to grow up to become a solitary creature, at her present stage of development, isolation was an unnatural condition.

Sibling attachment served the species. The strong bonds the littermates had developed prevented them from dispersing in the absence of their mother. It insured that both kittens would be on hand to receive a share of whatever food she dragged back to them. The two siblings also kept one another warm and occupied, exercised and entertained. Now, the little female experienced separation from her brother as painful. When self-grooming brought her no comfort, she began to complain in a loud voice.

Unlike her brother's water-muffled cries, her piercing wails were heard by her mother, who, feeling rested at last, quit her sleep-

ing niche and located her offspring. The two animals greeted by touching noses and brushing sides. Then they curled together and the baby nursed.

If the adult female noted the absence of her firstborn, the observation did not immediately interfere with the care she now gave to the kitten at her breast. When the baby had suckled, she rolled her over and thoroughly licked away all the debris and mud acquired during the day's adventures. When this was done, she stood up, stretched each leg to its full extension, yawned, then strolled into a patch of reeds. In rapid succession, she stalked and consumed three voles, none of which did she offer to her offspring. When she killed a fourth one, however, she brought it to her baby, whose nutritional needs for that day had by no means been met. The kitten quickly devoured the mouse headfirst and felt the better for it.

The mother bobcat now began to call. She sounded like a bleating goat—*maa, maa, maa!* Clearly, she was trying to summon her absent kitten from whatever place of concealment he had found too pleasant to leave. When he did not appear, the mother bobcat's cries grew more strident and punctuated the canyon's quiet like the complaints of some agitated raven. Up and down the bank she paced, entoning her distress. In and out of the vegetation she searched for her missing baby, but none of her efforts conjured up the kitten she sought. At last she sat down and began to groom herself. For a time, the act of licking her shoulders shifted her attention away from her anxiety, but her distress was too intense, too persistent to be dissipated with the stroke of her tongue, and it soon resurfaced. For a long time she sat quietly, listened, and waited.

When her male kitten failed to put in an appearance, the female bobcat at last rose and began to meander downstream. Her remaining kitten pranced after her. The two visited an old scat pile situated beside a fallen branch, one the mother bobcat had created some two years before while attempting to raise another pair of kittens in this place. Now she clawed at the whitened stools until they dissolved into chalk. Then she carefully positioned herself and defecated on top of the old sign. Her kitten watched, and then she, too, defecated a few feet to one side. Unlike her mother, however, the kitten did not leave her pile of stools exposed, but scraped loose dirt over it. Since the day the two baby bobcats had been carried out of their rocky den and dropped onto loose soil, both had fastidiously clawed earth over their urine and feces. Each performed this act instinctively, without first having to observe it done by their mother. All that had been necessary to elicit the behavior was the feel of dirt beneath their paws.

When her scat posting had been updated, the mother bobcat began threading her way through the willow stand. She paused frequently and listened. Twice she called. Her behavior left little doubt that she was still searching for her missing kitten. When no answering wail directed her to his whereabouts, she finally resumed hunting.

The sound of available rodents scurrying in the brush was a distraction that the underfed cat could not easily ignore. Now she stalked them in the sedge while her remaining kitten trailed behind her, imitating her every posture. This was the youngster's first lesson in searching out prey, and the adult bobcat seemed cognizant of the importance of the event. At times she even appeared to instruct her offspring in an intentional manner, for whenever her baby failed to walk quietly or moved when she should have held still, the mother cat turned and gave her a long look. This stare so disconcerted the little bobcat that she would freeze in her tracks. On the other hand, when the kitten lost interest or lagged too far behind, the mother cat halted and waggled her stubby tail as if beckoning her baby to hurry along. Thus, without benefit of spoken language, the mother bobcat taught her young one the necessity of stealth when searching for prey.

All night, up and down the bank, the pair hunted. At one point they wandered near enough to where the male kitten was stranded to have caught sight of him, had he been able to attract their attention. But he could not. Although he spied their shadowy forms slipping in and out of the willow stand, his small voice could no longer produce a sound. His strength was spent, and, despite his highly evolved sense of balance, his body began to sway.

The coup de grace came out of the night sky. A short-eared owl, hunting the stream gulch, spied the kitten and made a low pass over his head. Bobcat was not a food item with which the crow-sized bird was familiar. Normally, its diet consisted of voles, frogs, sometimes even a weasel. Though the raptor would very likely eschew the stranded and helpless kitten, once identified, it nevertheless made a second low pass to take a closer look.

However great had been the kitten's fear during his long siege on the rock, this was of small account compared to the terror that

gripped and crippled him now as the dark bird swooped over his head. His fright was primordial, unlearned, a response to overhead shadows written into the genes of every cat. Perhaps some winged and ancient creature, some flying pterosaur, once preyed on the miacid ancestor of the family Felidae. Whatever the origin of his terrible dread, the kitten cringed, pulled in his head, and, in so doing, lost his balance and slid into the black water.

In a second the current sucked him under, carried him off. For seventy-five yards he bobbed and struggled until the stream shifted course and turned a sharp bend. There the kitten was deposited on a mound of debris which, like himself, had failed to make it round the turn.

For some time he lay on the pileup of weeds and sticks and made futile swimming motions with his legs. When at last he began to trust that the muck beneath him would not suck him under, he stopped paddling and pulled himself on to a rock. He was debilitated, in need of the warm body of his mother. Only her attention, her milk, and her maternal energy could revive him now.

But the rushing stream had placed him outside of his mother's normal range, had dropped him on the opposite bank on ground occupied by another female bobcat. His mother would not find him here, for only on rare occasions did she encroach on her neighbor's domain.

The male kitten was not the first baby she had lost. All the kittens born to her over the course of her reproductive life had either died or disappeared. Although each loss had distressed her, inevitably she had rallied and forgotten each painful experience. The instinct for survival was strong in the female bobcat. Even now she was beginning to grow reconciled to the absence of the male kitten. Though he had by no means faded from her memory, she directed all of her attention to the offspring who was still in tow.

Chapter 8

From a distance, the dark green juniper appeared shrublike, though it was a twelve-foot-tall tree. Its feathery foliage, hugging twisting stems, gave it the dense look of a bush. Its lowest boughs grew close to the ground and spread wide, like some great sage hen's wings awkwardly trying to shelter the round-bodied rabbit brush that grew around its base.

For more than a century, the juniper had stood alone, a single tree surrounded by desert brush. Boring beetles invaded its dead branches, sage thrashers ate its silver blue berries, winter mantled it. Still it lived on. Its solitariness was awesome. Shoshone hunters long ago had made camp near the tree and, moved by its presence, imbued it with a spirit god. Then they passed from the scene. Still the tree stood, untouched by the sweep of such human events. Since then, wind, silence, and time weighed on the ancient tree, and no person heard the creak of its branches or watched it put forth green fingers.

The tree was known to a bobcat, however. It was, in fact, an important feature on her home range. Frequently, she visited it to sharpen her claws, shredding its fibrous trunk down to vulnerable cambium. After each assault, the tree slowly repaired itself, building a new shield of bark. Then the bobcat would return and repeat the mischief.

It was necessary for the old cat to hone her talons, to keep them razor sharp. They were her grappling hooks, her means of escaping up trees, of scaling rock faces. They were also her carving tools, used to rip open prey she killed. And most important, sharp claws were the bobcat's best defense against enemies. When under attack, she

could roll onto her back and rake her adversary with this exquisite weaponry.

Such vital equipment required maintenance. To prevent them from wearing blunt, the cat walked with her claws withdrawn, protected in sheaths of skin. This was their natural, relaxed position; to extend them, muscular exertion was required. Moreover, because they never ceased to grow, their old and worn outer layers frequently had to be scaled away, a task best accomplished by dragging them down a stump or a tree.

For that purpose, the old female often made use of the juniper, and had done so for many years. Like the tree, she was a survivor, the oldest bobcat within a fifty-mile radius. Over the course of her life, as her less invincible neighbors died off, she had expanded her range to include portions of theirs. Now, her irregularly shaped polygram claim measured eighteen square miles. But she was land poor. Despite the size of her holdings, rabbits were in short supply here as everywhere. As a result, like her neighbor to the west, she had failed to raise kittens over the past few years.

This "tree bobcat" had a distinguishing feature—a bobbed tail that was somewhat longer than those sported by most of her kind. The peculiarity had not shown up in a single one of the thirty-three offspring she had borne during her fifteen years of life. Even had the trait been a dominant one, however, it would not have made much of a mark on the bobcat population here in southern Idaho. Only nine of her progeny had survived to be one year old, and of these nine, only two had lived to the age of five. Life is hard on the young of animals who stand at the top of the food chain.

One of the tree bobcat's two surviving progeny was now her neighbor, the female who had recently led her kittens to the stream bed. This daughter was seldom sighted by the tree bobcat, despite

the fact that the animals' ranges were contiguous. Yet each kept apprised of the other by making regular checks on one another's scent stations. Recently, the stream bobcat's postings had informed the tree bobcat that she had borne kittens. Traces of lactose could be detected in her waste.

The old bobcat had herself given birth to kittens in May, her twelfth litter. Three perfect babies were born in a rock shelter not far from the juniper tree. Life in this natal den had been sweet for her young. The tree bobcat was a gentle and solicitous mother, and if her infant kittens had had a single complaint to make, it would probably have been of too much maternal grooming.

But in the world of the wildcat, good mothering does not insure the survival of offspring. The female was also charged with the responsibility of being a provider, and the old cat was no longer so adept at this task. Though she made strenuous efforts to search out rabbits, often traveling great distances from her den to do so, more often than not her hunting forays were unsuccessful. When she returned, her teething kittens had to be content with an unrelieved diet of milk and a vigorous grooming. What the developing carnivores needed was meat.

Had the bobcat possessed the coyote mother's trick of carrying food in her stomach and regurgitating it upon her return to her den, she likely would have shared more of her catches with her kittens. Dragging a jackrabbit carcass across miles of rough and broken country was difficult work and required energy that the old cat no longer possessed. More often than not, she halted midway and ate her kill.

Or had the old female, like her daughter to the west, possessed the ingenuity or good luck to seek and find alternative food, had she begun to hunt grouse and pack rats in earnest, her babies still might have thrived. She was, however, too advanced in age to adapt her ways. Imprinted on her memory was at least a decade of rabbit abundance. Imprinted on her racial memory was a predator-prey association that extended back in time perhaps two million years. Her urge to stalk and kill rabbits was primordial and compulsive. And though she was sufficiently opportunistic to kill any species she happened upon, she made no deliberate effort to search out alternative prey of sufficient size to meet her kittens' increasing needs. Instead, she returned to the places where her memory told her that rabbits were once abundant. They no longer were.

The female kitten was the first to die. She did not actually starve. As her nutritional needs failed to be met, her resistance to infection dropped, an abscess appeared on her gum, and her face swelled. Then, because eating aggravated her painful mouth, she abstained from nursing and her body grew weak. Finally, unable to combat the spreading bacteria, she died.

That night the tree bobcat moved her two surviving kittens, both males, to a new den. The place she chose was located on an alluvial fan that sloped from the base of the mountain, a well-vegetated ramp built from gravel and sediment that had washed off the mountainside over countless centuries. Here and there, tips of bedrock still protruded, and in one of these andesite outcroppings she settled her babies.

To all outward appearances, the north-facing incline seemed devoid of water, yet an abundance of life in the area suggested otherwise. Yellow jackets and bee flies circled and droned. A chipmunk seated upon a sage bush stiffened and sounded a long buzzing alarm call when the three bobcats padded into view. During the wet weeks of early spring, the sandy soil had soaked up mountain runoff. By now this water would not have been accessible, would have been trapped in deep underground pockets, had it not been for the work of two coyotes who, smelling it, tunneled down through four feet of earth to enjoy a long drink. Afterward, many species were able to avail themselves of the life-sustaining substance.

The pair of coyotes had worked cooperatively. One had burrowed while the other, following close behind, had kicked to the surface all the dirt his partner had loosened. When they struck water, both satisfied their thirst, backed out of the tunnel, shook their coats clean, and departed at a brisk trot. They never again visited the site of all their labor.

The well they had created quickly transformed the biotic character of the slope. Birds and insects hovered in the area. Rodent populations burgeoned. Even a spadefoot toad mysteriously turned up one day at the mouth of the well. Some of these creatures would soon supply the tree bobcat with the bait she needed to teach her young to kill. For her two remaining kittens had reached the age when such lessons should begin.

The two kittens were not equally endowed. Despite the fact that each had enjoyed undisputed claim to a private nursing nipple on their mother's body, one had outstripped the other in physical growth and was the more apt hunting pupil as well. The very first live mouse presented to him, he killed. At the instant it was released, he pounced on the luckless victim, and when his brother tried to join in the game, the introduction of this competitive element so excited the firstborn kitten that he performed the fatal bite with no further delay.

Nevertheless, he was not yet a hunter. Before he could begin to obtain food for himself, he needed much practice at locating, stalking, and capturing prey, skills that could only be acquired through experience. His mother dutifully supplied him and his brother with practice bait, but the firstborn kitten killed and consumed nearly every mouse or vole she delivered. Thus, despite the rabbit shortage, he continued to thrive, while his outcompeted brother failed to acquire either hunting proficiency or much to eat.

For a full week the bobcat family remained at the coyote well. Then, quite abruptly, the tree bobcat began to take her young on nocturnal hunting expeditions. Often they traveled too far to return to their starting point and so would remain for a day or two wherever they happened to find themselves. The old female, being thoroughly familiar with her range, knew of many places where three cats could hide.

One day she led them back to the old juniper tree. The kittens, more mobile now than when they had left this place, no longer felt any compulsion to remain near the rock pile that had served as their natal den. Now they explored a wide area and discovered the tree. Nothing they had yet encountered in their young lives so intrigued them. The rough texture of bark felt good to their paws as they dragged their tiny claws across the base of the trunk. When the firstborn decided to make an ascent, his brother was right behind him. Up the tree the two kittens climbed, their front paws splayed wide and clinging, their strong hind legs providing them with boosts.

Like children who like to play under furniture, the kittens seemed to enjoy the intimacy of life inside a tree. With unshakable confidence, they walked swaying branches many times their height above the ground. Coming down was more challenging. They could not descend headfirst like a squirrel; their weight would put too much strain on their inverted claws. Had they possessed the flexible ankle joint of their cousins to the south—the margay and the ocelot—they could have rotated their feet and made a headlong descent. But the bobcat was not so perfectly adapted to arboreal life

as these other members of the cat family. So they lowered themselves backward, letting go briefly to drop a few inches, then, after each short slide, stabbing at the trunk with their tiny grappling hooks.

When prey declined around the natal den, the mother cat responded properly and moved her babies before all rodent breeding stock was consumed. In a few weeks' time, should she return, the area would be repopulated with rodents. Meanwhile, she conducted her kittens to a cutting in the desert, a place where heavy machinery, designed to carry and erect power lines, had torn up the ground.

To repair the damage done here, nature would require decades of time. All the climax vegetation—the bluebunch wheatgrass and the three-tip sage—had been destroyed, and now a succession of annual plants—cheatgrass, needle and thread, and greasewood—had invaded. Along with these poor-quality plants had sprung up a high population of rodents.

The old bobcat, committed though she was to a diet of rabbit, nonetheless was an opportunistic hunter. When presented with an abundant food source, she exploited it. And now she followed the power line, pouncing on the mice that proliferated in its swath. Her kittens trailed behind her, the firstborn male catching three out of every ten creatures he stalked.

The accident occurred at the top of a rise. A wooden pole had been temporarily erected to prop up sagging high-voltage wires that cleared the crest of a rise by only a few feet. Elsewhere across the desert, the power lines were strung high, draped on evenly spaced tall metal structures. The prop pole, being made of wood, was irresistible to the bobcats. The old female ran to it and immediately began to sharpen her claws. Her kittens shimmied to the top.

Their deaths were instantaneous. One moment they were alive, learning, growing, taking in life's impressions. Then they were dead, insentient, gone. The old female grieved, remaining near the dropped bodies of her kittens all day and throughout the night. In the morning she tried to arouse them by presenting their tiny corpses with live mice.

But the young bobcats would chase no more rodents. Their promise of life had been broken.

Chapter 9

When the tree bobcat finally grew resigned to the loss of her kittens, she headed for the streambed. She traveled at night and at a leisurely pace, stopping from time to time to stalk and capture small rodents. In the pale light of a full moon, nocturnal animals, while no more abundant than at other times, appeared so, for they were more visible and probably more active.

The cat saw everything. Her eyes were perfectly adapted to gather low-level illumination, and no crepuscular form escaped her attention. Her pupils were capable of wide dilation, and light-gathering crystals in her retina amplified what stray light there was. When the moon beamed directly on the cat's night-adapted eyes, these retinal mirrors shone like blue-green jewels; in daylight, the tree bobcat's eyes were a common yellow.

When she arrived at the stream, the old cat took a long drink. Some time had passed since she had savored the taste of water. Normally, the prey she consumed contained sufficient fluid to satisfy her needs, but since the death of her kittens, she had departed from her usual practice of holing up during the intense heat of the day. As a result, vapor loss from her lungs, her tongue, and her paw pads had begun to exceed a safe level. Salts and urea were collecting in her body in poisonous concentrations. To compensate for so much evaporation, she now consumed water to the point of discomfort.

As she lapped, the damp ground beneath her feet felt soothing to her hot paw pads. When at last she was satisfied, she waded into the shallows. A fish gliding among the stones seized her attention, and, with a flat paw, she smacked the water's surface and created a rain of spray that startled several rainbow trout idling nearby. Their

sudden and frenetic dartings in turn excited the cat, and in a single leap, she positioned herself midstream, atop a boulder that offered a view of the underwater circus.

Watching fish was a pleasurable pastime for the old bobcat. The trouts' scales, ribbons of color in daylight, shone like mica-flecked rocks in the moonlight. From time to time, she took a swipe at the gleaming forms, causing them to shoot off like fireworks in every direction. But after a few such assaults, the trout moved to a new location and the bobcat was forced to look for other fish to harry. Leaping lightly from boulder to boulder, she managed to disturb six species—mountain whitefish, char, kokanee salmon, sculpin, and both rainbow and brook trout.

The old cat knew perfectly well how to catch a fish. She had taught herself how to do it. When her instinctive rabbit-stalking movements had proved useless in an aquatic element, she had tried other strategies. Whenever one met with success, she incorporated it into her modus operandi. She had discovered, for example, that a light tap on the water would sometimes bring one of the insect-feeding species to the surface. From then on she "fished" in the true sense of the word, luring victims to her lethal claws in the same way sportsmen use their casting rods. When a victim was deceived by her ruse, she would bat it onto the bank and dispatch it quickly with a series of hard bites before it could flop its way back to a watery domain. She learned the hard way that hooking a fish twice was as difficult a feat as bringing down a bird once it had taken wing.

But on this night the old cat was not serious about capturing the sinuous forms with which she toyed. More than food, she was seeking "relief play." For several days, while mourning her kittens, she had remained quiet. Now her central nervous system craved exhilaration. And like the untimely burst of laughter that sometimes follows shock in human beings, the cat's mood altered abruptly. Suddenly she began jumping about like a fawn.

What fantasies played across her brain as she capered about in the fabulous light could hardly have been more surrealistic than the effect her performance would have created on a casual observer. Leaping from boulder to boulder like some giddy phantasma, she might well have been performing a magical rite. And in a way, she was, for this spontaneous activity was stimulating her endocrine system, helping to restore to it a more normal homeostasis. Self-excitation was therapeutic, a medicine dance, a tonic.

At daybreak, the bobcat's waltzing silhouette grew rosy with detail and her madcap antics slowed and came to a halt. When the sweet warble of a sage thrasher bounced off the canyon wall, she climbed onto the bank. It was a new day, one that would alter the course of her remaining life.

She noticed the half-dead kitten at the same moment the sun lit up the rocky gorge. She did not approach it at once, but seated herself some thirty yards away and waited. When time passed, however, and the strange feline failed to comply with the rules of bobcat etiquette and depart the area, she advanced cautiously. Keeping her eyes fixed on the limp body, she twice circled it, then moved close enough to make contact.

The male kitten, when he felt a wet nose gently probing his own dry one, opened his eyes, and a faint purr pulsated in his throat. And this kitten song aroused in the old female a recollection of her own lost young. She answered with a kind of quizzical sound, a long vowel tone.

But something was not right. Something about the little castaway disturbed her, and, unpredictably, she grew hostile. Like a prankster who springs at a child and shouts "boo," she suddenly jumped at the kitten while simultaneously emitting an explosive "huff" sound.

The kitten, too weak to heed this feline warning and take flight, closed his eyes and relapsed into a state of semiconsciousness. The old bobcat studied him. His unresponsiveness baffled her, perhaps even reminded her of her own dead kittens. She moved closer and sniffed his limp body, but the baby's scent was foreign and caused her to draw back. For several minutes she did nothing, as if awaiting some cue from the little stranger that would resolve her ambivalence. When the kitten remained still, the tree bobcat was at an impasse. Finally, she permitted herself one last inspection, this time sniffing the kitten's anal region. Then, almost mechanically, she began to groom him, vigorously dragging her tongue down his side and across his belly.

Maternal attention was exactly what the languishing kitten needed, and he responded to the tongue massage with a feeble purr. This sound once again stirred something deep, something primal, in the old bobcat and even caused milk to let down in her breasts. The kitten, picking up the scent of lactose, raised his head and with treading paws sought a plucked teat, and this infantile gesture was the single move that the old cat could not resist. Slowly she lowered

herself over his body, and, as her milk began to flow, so all ambivalence drained from her psyche. The alien kitten was accepted.

The kitten had a tonic effect on the old bobcat, revitalized her in some way, just as rain sometimes puts life back into a parched flower. Her muscles became supple, her blood quickened. No less salutary was the effect that the tree bobcat produced on the youngster: He thrived under her care. It was an alliance like those said to be made in heaven, for each animal needed what the other could give.

In short order, the kitten controlled the old bobcat. When she withdrew to hunt or to relieve herself, he wrinkled up his flat face and complained. And when she returned, he rewarded her with purrs and shoulder brushes. Suffering as he was, not from illness but from exposure, maternal attention was the only medicine he required to set him right, and this remedy he artlessly sought and received.

Though he was well past an age to be shown such deference, he even succeeded in obtaining ready-killed prey from his new guardian. Normally, the mice a female bobcat delivered to a ten-week-old kitten would be alive and squeaking. Less surprising was the old cat's readiness to groom her charge. The demonstrative old mother washed him so assiduously that his fur stuck up in points and his nerves tingled.

All this attention, of course, hastened his recovery. In just a few days the kitten gained back his strength and the pair departed the area, wending their way along the stream to a place where the water disappeared underground. Beyond this desert sink, the dry, pebbly bottom of a once extensive waterway stretched onward for several miles, one of nature's ruins. In the immediate vicinity of the sink stood thickets of reeds and brambles, and stagnant seepages dotted the stony basin, providing breeding pools for mayflies and toads. Voles and chipmunks and skinks and Jerusalem crickets were also abundant here, all useful creatures to an unpracticed hunter.

The male kitten stalked the reeds, investigating this new world with the self-assurance of a grown cat. Pouncing on a Jerusalem cricket was an event. The huge insect propelled itself about in a manner that could be described as neither flight nor leap, but which contained an element of unpredictability that never failed to excite the kitten. The young bobcat, ever alert to the rasping announcements of cricket presences, soared after them.

Feathers offered another kind of pleasure. A primary from the wing of a red-tailed hawk, when batted, sallied about erratically, like a leaf in a crosswind. Manipulating such objects was important to the male kitten's development, improving his dexterity and eye-paw coordination.

One day the young bobcat dislodged a stone and unearthed a skink, turning the blue-tailed lizard out of hiding. He studied the creature intently. Glazed scales on its head and back were handsomely decorated with black, yellow, and brown stripes. Its tail was a piece of sky. The reptile responded to the disruption of its peace by flicking its long tongue and blinking. It had been caught off guard, and now it utilized all its sharp senses to identify the nature of the invasion. While its tongue tested the air for stray molecules, its eyes scanned the immediate environs for a crevice in which to escape. It saw everything. Even in the millisecond that it took the amazing lizard to blink, it continued to monitor the kitten's whereabouts; windows built into its lower eyelids permitted this uninterrupted vision.

It was the kitten who made the first move. With his paw he gently shoved the skink in an arc across the ground. In a flash, the reptile reared and nipped him in the paw. Though no real harm was done, the pinch hurt and surprised the young bobcat, causing him to jump backward and shake his forefoot.

Although he had been very young at the time of the incident, the kitten had a dim recollection of his mother's violent struggle with the rattlesnake. Now he associated that memory with the skink and the bite he had just sustained, and his mother's fierce reaction to reptiles became his own fixed attitude. Rage, a new feeling, generated energy in him that pressured for expression, and he struck with claws fully extended, using his longest reach. But the skink was fast and shot off on tiny legs that seemed to work as rapidly as

wing flutters. Before it could reach the refuge of a rock crevice, however, the kitten had lunged and landed on its bright blue tail.

Still, the skink was not defeated. For the lizard possessed a defense not bequeathed to the mammalian world, and, with a snap, it freed itself of both its tail and its captor. Then it darted into brush, none the worse for the loss of two inches of renewable length.

For several seconds the dumbstruck kitten remained locked in position, trying to reconcile the piece of tail, still securely pinned under his paw, with the animal that had just escaped. At last he straightened up and examined his worthless booty. Then he promptly discarded it, and, with a cat's show of indifference, he turned his attention to the condition of his coat. For a quarter of an hour, he groomed his fur. Mastering the hunt would take the young kitten many months to learn, but mastering defeat he already understood. In the world of the wildcat, dwelling on failure could only prove counterproductive.

Chapter 10

By now the male kitten knew how to kill. He had not, however, acquired this skill without special priming from his stepmother. Once, when the live mice she brought him failed to excite him sufficiently to generate a nape bite, she had reconfiscated one of her offerings and played with it herself. This so agitated the kitten that he acted assertively, recovered the mouse, and killed it immediately. After that he knew what to do with the training prey he was served.

Ten days after that milestone had been passed, he experienced a hunting setback when he pounced on a grasshopper mouse. The chunky rodent looked no more threatening than did the voles and deer mice with which he was familiar. But the grasshopper mouse was a formidable fighter, a meat eater who pursued and fed on many of the same creatures the bobcat hunted. Deer mice, voles, pocket gophers, kangaroo rats, snakes, even his own brethren were ordinary fare for this pint-sized predator. Fearlessly, it scent-trailed victims into their own holes, where, with sixteen exquisitely sharp teeth, it crushed their skulls.

The kitten, having just gained sufficient self-confidence to set out on food searches by himself, reacted with high excitement at the discovery of the cinnamon-colored mouse seated under sagebrush, placidly beheading a grasshopper. Slowly, imperceptibly, the kitten flattened himself to the ground and waited for a propitious moment to strike. In anticipation of the event, his hind feet began to tread the ground.

The mouse had finished dining and was in the process of cleaning its whiskers when the bobcat's containment exploded, catapulting him into a yellow and gray arc. When the cat landed, pinned

under his two oversized front paws was one grasshopper mouse. Had he killed his victim at once, crushed its vertebrae with a tooth, all would have been well. But the kitten wanted to play with his captive, and so he released the formidable little rodent.

In an instant, it leaped up and, screeching loudly, attached itself to the bobcat's ear. Now it was the kitten's turn to shriek, and his caterwauls were heard by the tree bobcat, who sprinted a hundred yards to his side. But she could do nothing to help him; the bobcat kitten could not hold still long enough to permit her assistance. Wildly, he jumped about trying to shake off his tormentor, while the old cat chased after him making matters worse.

Even more intolerable to the kitten than the pain he was enduring was the unshakable nature of the attacker. Again and again, he clawed at his ear, swatted at the mouse. But it clung like a stickleburr and seemed impervious to all punishment. At last, though, the

kitten managed to strike such a blow that his tiny adversary was flung to the ground, still gripping a piece of ear tissue in its teeth. Instantly, before it had time to fly at the kitten's head again, the old tree bobcat killed and ate it.

For several days afterward, the tree bobcat licked the kitten's wounded ear, cleaning out the maggot eggs laid in it by flies, which unerringly find such open sores. In the absence of a sterile cleansing agent, the cat's tongue prevented larvae from hatching in the lesions, but its rasplike surface irritated the festering injury. Eventually, a lick granuloma developed, which was slow to heal, and, as a consequence, the kitten's ear pinna bore a permanent nick, a characteristic that would henceforth distinguish him from all other bobcats.

Cleansing his wound revived in the old bobcat her passion for grooming, for mothering young, an impulse that had begun to wane as her charge had matured. As a result, the bond between the two animals was revitalized. When not licking one another, the pair touched noses, rubbed cheeks, or butted foreheads, and in so doing they anointed one another with the secretions produced by glands located on their lips and foreheads. What these perfumes implied, only a bobcat could know, but one thing was certain: no natural mother lavished more attention on her own youngster. The two had become inseparable.

No longer did the nick-eared kitten wait at the sink for the tree bobcat to return from her rabbit hunts. Now "Nick Ear" accompanied her. He was old enough to range many miles without growing tired, and the two cats frequently shifted their hunting site. Their never-ending search for scarce rabbits, however, burned precious fuel, and every failed hunting venture further depleted the physical reserves that their efforts were meant to replenish. The bobcats had to know when to quit, when to be satisfied with less than a full stomach. While such a condition could be tolerated during mild weather, soon the temperature would plummet and additional calories would be required just to keep warm. In preparation for this periodic metabolic drain, the bobcats should have been putting on an extra layer of fat. This year, however, no such reserve was being stored. During the best of times, life at the top of the food chain was precarious; for the bobcats, it would soon be the worst of times.

Chapter 11

The coyotes were in full voice again. For weeks, since the birth of their young, the wild canids had kept silent, thereby safeguarding the location of their dens. Now their pups were old enough to be initiated into the raptures of the howl, and at dusk their songs erupted from a dozen locations in the desert as pack after pack joined in. Falsetto notes in particular prompted the young of the year to add their squeaky ululations to the antiphonal chorus. In summer, voles were plentiful, the weather was fine, and life was worth celebrating.

The tree bobcat listened attentively to the nightly rhapsodizing and registered the coyotes' whereabouts. She avoided leading her adopted kitten near these places. Although in one-to-one combat she would be more than a match for a coyote, the young kitten might be vulnerable prey. A pair of coyotes acting together could even make short work of her. By the same token, any untended coyote pup she chanced upon would stand little chance of escaping the killing bite she would likely inflict on it. The perpetuation of *Canis latrans* and *Lynx rufus* depends on the long period of protection that adult members of both species provide their young.

At the same time, neither the coyote nor the bobcat went out of its way to make trouble for the other. Instinctively, each seemed to recognize that doing battle with an opponent of comparable strength and poor palatability was pointless. Proof of their ability to coexist in close proximity was their long history of doing so. The two animals had evolved together and thrived over eons of time without doing one another harm. Pressured by one another's competitive demands on the environment, each had successfully

95

adapted itself to a slightly different niche in the same general habitat.

Coyotes raised their young in open terrain, excavating burrows under the shallow roots of sagebrush. Bobcats holed up in natural caves or in rock piles where the surrounding ground was too hard for a coyote to dig. As a result, though the two animals consumed many of the same prey species, neither depleted the food supply in the other's immediate living space. Moreover, while their food preferences were often the same, they were differently ordered. In summer, coyotes devoured a great quantity of meadow voles and deer mice. If these rodents were in good supply, the opportunistic canids often did not exert themselves to course after bounding rabbits. When they did pursue lagomorphs, coyotes, being sight hunters, would more often run down the long-legged jackrabbit. The bobcat, on the other hand, lacking endurance, limited its chases to short sprints. The bobcat preferred to surprise its prey at close range and, as a result, captured a disproportionate number of the smaller, slower cottontails.

Nor was the coyote so finicky an eater as was the bobcat, and as a consequence, it more frequently fed on carrion. The coyote would watch the sky for circling ravens and magpies to alert it to the location of a dead animal. Then it would hie itself to the site of their food find and dine in the midst of the flock. These birds would not tolerate a bobcat feeding alongside them, nor would a bobcat be inclined to seek out such ripe meat as the ravens and the coyotes found acceptable fare. Still, the bobcat's preference for fresh kills was not entirely a matter of its more discriminating palate. The bobcat was driven by a biological need to hunt. At certain intervals, an urge to chase and capture lively moving objects mounted in its nervous system and demanded outlet. At such times, dead, immobile animals held little fascination for it. A bobcat scavenged when necessary but preferred—indeed, was compelled by its very nature—to hunt.

So it happened that a family of coyotes inhabited the tree bobcat's range and the paths of the two species seldom crossed. Three pups had been born to a fawn-colored bitch only a week before the old bobcat had given birth to her litter. At eleven days of age the young canids had emerged from their underground chamber for the first time. Not until then did their mother permit her mate, a rufous-tinged dog of some vintage, to make their acquaintance.

From the day of their birth, the male had been keenly aware of the pups' existence, had smelled their traces on his mate's body. When she barred him from entering the tunnel that led to their natal chamber, however, he had had to suppress his investigative impulses. Despite this frustration, he continued to provide food for the nursing bitch, sharing with her, twice daily, the contents of his full stomach.

The female accepted her mate's donations as her due and kept him away from her litter. Even when belowground, she was able to sense his approach and would emerge and intercept him at some distance from her den. There, the pair would greet with the enthusiasm dogs show returning owners. The female was the more demonstrative. She wagged her tail with such energy that her entire back end would sway. Then she would lick the muzzle of the more restrained male until, unable to contain himself, he would regurgitate all the voles and mice he had spent the day capturing. These she would hastily consume. Nursing three pups gave her a ravenous appetite.

Then, one bright morning, one by one, the chocolate-colored

pups climbed out of their dark underground home and began bouncing about in the sunlight. At that moment, their protective mother signaled her mate to come meet the family. With unconcealed enthusiasm, he sprang to the den mound and began inspecting each one of his three offspring with his long, pointed nose, licking and bowling them about until their scents and looks and squeals were imprinted on his memory. It was important that he become thoroughly familiar with these small creatures, whose demands for solid food would steadily escalate over the next few weeks. The male coyote would be one of their chief providers. Unlike the male bobcat, he would enjoy no leisure season in spring.

When the pups were one month old, their mother moved them to a freshly dug burrow, free of the fleas and flies that inevitably collect on scraps of food left about a natal den. From this, their second home, they began to go on short excursions, exploring limited areas of their new environment. They never strayed far, however. Until they could be assembled by means of a vocal call, the youngsters obediently remained wherever their parents left them.

Howling would liberate them. Their nightly singing sessions, besides providing an expressive outlet for their ebullient spirits, served to acquaint each pup with the distinctive voice of each parent. After this information had been assimilated, family members

could disperse and assemble at will, communicating their where-abouts to one another vocally. Since neighboring packs also engaged in evening songfests, the voices of nonpack animals were also learned and later would not be confused with those of the family.

By summer the pups were being taken by one or both parents on long excursions into a wide world. Special places where voles and deer mice abounded were revealed to them. They also learned to drink at the clear stream which flowed from the mountain and watered a few miles of desert before vanishing underground.

One day one of the pups set off on his own in the direction of this sink. Heretofore, he had visited the place only in the company of one of his parents. Perhaps some recollection of mousing success at the site now prompted this, his first solo expedition. At twelve weeks of age, he was already adept at catching voles and mice. In typical coyote fashion, he would freeze in a point, like a hunting dog, whenever a rustle in the vegetation indicated the presence of prey. Then, when the moment seemed right, he would leap high in the air, jackknife, and come down with all his force on his two front legs. If his aim was accurate, the unfortunate object of this aerial feat would find itself pinned under his forepaws.

Upon arrival at the sink, the pup headed for one of the stagnant water holes which daily decreased in size and number during the heat of August. Alternately, he lapped and scooped water with his trowel-like underjaw, and he did not at first notice the flat-faced creature who was standing on a rock watching him. But something alerted him. Mid-lap, the coyote pup raised his head and let the water dribble from his open mouth. Facing him was an animal larger than any prey he had yet seen; it was the same size as himself, yet it was not a coyote. The pup responded by opening his mouth to its full flex and exposing all thirty-two of his sharp baby teeth.

The bobcat kitten was not impressed by this gape, for the body signals of a coyote were not in his feline vocabulary. Down he climbed from the slab of lava rock which had served as his lookout post and slowly he advanced toward the coyote pup.

The young coyote hunched and rounded his spine in the manner of a Halloween cat. But even this posture, so well understood by coyotes and foxes and, indeed, by most species of the world's cats, failed to deter the oncoming kitten. The bobcat's threat posture was different. The bobcat expressed aggression by raising his shoulders and presenting, not an enlarged view of his side, but his full face, which, at maturity, would be enhanced by wide muttonchops. In this, he behaved like a maned lion. So the bobcat did not take offense at the coyote's behavior. His mood, in fact, was genial, a fact that could easily have been discerned by another bobcat, for he walked boldly, with his stubby tail held erect.

Now it was the coyote pup who misread the bobcat's mood. He understood the cat's posture in terms of his own species' behavior. To the coyote, a stiffly held tail signaled hostility. A coyote who wished to communicate friendly intentions did so by carrying his tail in a low, swinging, relaxed position. Accordingly, the pup's hostility now escalated, and he tipped his head to one side the better to expose his long double row of teeth. But even this exaggerated display of dentition did not deter the oncoming kitten, whose unshakable confidence unnerved the coyote. The pup rolled onto his back and assumed a posture of abject submission.

In the more social world of the wild coyote, this act of surrender would have been understood for what it was—a ritualized gesture of appeasement, a technique for defusing aggression. Nick Ear, however, did not understand this conciliatory language; his species did not possess it. The young bobcat was destined to become a solitary animal who would seldom enjoy contact with his own kind. Even his associations with future mates would be brief, lasting but a few days each year. The bobcat's method of maintaining peace, therefore, was to avoid other bobcats, and the sociable coyote's sophisticated body language was lost on him.

Not that the bobcat kitten lacked communicative signals appropriate to his needs. Prolonged dependence on his mother necessitated that he, too, possess a body language. Littermates could express mood and interpret intention by means of facial expressions, tail positions, and back angles. Mother bobcats, moreover, could employ a wide range of vocal sounds to direct, call, and correct their young. Nevertheless, being that social contact among adults was limited, appeasement had never become a part of the species' repertoire. Thus, the male kitten was not equipped to read the meaning of the coyote's upturned body, and he interpreted the posture to be an aggressive maneuver. A warring cat, after all, would flip onto its back to rake an opponent with its hind claws. The kitten, having no means of knowing that the supine creature before him possessed no such weaponry on his hind feet, responded

by backing away.

The coyote pup, now satisfied that his gesture of surrender had disarmed the stranger, sprang to his feet and prepared to participate in friendly greeting. His amicable move greatly alarmed the bobcat, and when the young canid raised his paw in typical canid invitation to play, Nick Ear went on the offensive. To the bobcat, a raised paw was a dangerous weapon, something to be respected. Nick Ear hunched his shoulders and ventilated his annoyance in a long, low, rumbling growl.

This unexpected response startled the pup, causing him to back away and sit down. He did understand a growl. He too employed that signal on occasion. For several minutes the two animals eyed one another, neither daring to make a move. Then the pup, feeling amiable again, expressed this attitude by wagging his ropy tail. The lashing appendage sent the kitten sprinting. In the bobcat's world, a twitching tail suggested mounting tension and aggressive intent.

The kitten took refuge on a high rock, and from that vantage place he hissed and spat at the coyote.

The standoff between the two species might well have lasted until the old tree bobcat returned from her rabbit hunt, had not a faraway wail alerted the young coyote that his clan was gathering for its evening howl. The call, unmistakably produced by his mother, was insistent and demanded a response. In a wavering voice, the little coyote tilted back his head and poured out his own rendition of the coyote song. Then he took off quickly, heading for the rendezvous site at a dead run.

After the coyote's departure, the kitten, curious about the strange creature with the pointed muzzle who behaved in so strange a manner, moved to where the pup had been seated and sniffed the ground. Perhaps, given time and freedom from parental constraint, the bobcat kitten and the coyote pup might have broken through the language barrier that separated the two species. The two animals shared many traits in common. Both possessed high intelligence, a playful spirit, curiosity, and the heart and courage that was the heritage of every predator. Ages ago they had spoken in the same voice, for both were descended from a common ancestor, one of the Miacidae. It was to this ancient creature that they owed their common membership in the order Carnivora.

But selective forces and differing environments had created changes, and long ago two variants on the same theme had survived to become the prototypes of the families Felidae and Canidae. Nor did.divergence stop there. In the end, the bobcat possessed so different a code of behavior from that of the coyote that neither was able to evaluate the mood or the intentions of the other.

FALL

Chapter 12

It was a day to fool migrating birds into delaying their flight plans. It was an Indian summer day, dazzling and blue. Even a horned lizard was abroad, deceived by the fair weather into emerging from a pile of loose soil into which it had burrowed during a two-week cold snap. The "horned toad," as this lizard is commonly called, needed the heat of the sun to energize its body. When days were chilly, its metabolism slowed, its appetite failed, and it pushed itself under a blanket of sandy loam. When winter arrived, it would remain underground, self-entombed, without benefit of food or sensory input. Not until spring, when the sun's radiant energy penetrated its dark burial site, would the lizard resurrect itself, pushing its way to the surface like some strange, fast-growing toadstool.

In appearance, the horned lizard was a relic from the age of the dinosaurs—a miniature dragon. Its body was covered with tiny, scaly projections. Attached to its fat, toadlike torso was a fringe of scaly daggers which could be laid flat or raised to a menacing angle, should a situation warrant. These pointed scales were the so-called horns for which the creature was named, but they were rarely used to jab anything. The horned lizard was singularly unaggressive, feeding almost entirely on ants, spiders, and sow bugs. Moreover, it seldom experienced the need to defend itself. What few predators were not put off by its unappealing appearance likely failed to notice the creature altogether, for it was well camouflaged, closely matching the color of whatever soil lay under its clawed feet. Most horned lizards were a dusty gray or tan, but some were clay colored, and a few, those that inhabited lava flows, were as black as obsidian.

The horned lizard's behavior was as unobtrusive as its appearance. Although it was active during the day, it scurried about so flattened to the ground that it scarcely cast a revealing shadow. At the first sign that its presence had been detected, it would stop dead in its tracks and remain motionless. In addition, the horned lizard possessed two bizarre defense mechanisms. When threatened, it could, by gulping air, puff itself up to menacing proportions. Should this stratagem fail to ward off attack, the lizard was capable of raising its own blood pressure to such a level that blood would spurt from its eye sockets, often for a distance of several feet.

Nevertheless, despite its protective coloration and shadowless existence, on this September day, the horned lizard had been spotted by the male kitten, who had, in fact, kept the reptile's movements under surveillance for several minutes. The young bobcat was in no hurry to arouse himself to inspect the animal more closely. A successful hunt during the night had satisfied his impulse to capture and play with prey, and the urge for more such activity might not come upon him again for several hours. Meanwhile, he enjoyed watching the horned lizard as it inched along behind an apparently endless column of ants, erasing the black line as it progressed.

Nick Ear reveled in the halcyon weather. Stretched out on the ground, he soaked in the sun's direct rays while simultaneously absorbing stored heat from the earth. From time to time, his drifting attention turned skyward, where violet-green swallows were dipping and skimming and performing aerial acrobatics as they fed on the light haze of insects that enveloped them. The flock was in migration after summering in Montana. Their stopover in the Idaho desert would be brief—an afternoon—for they had been late in arriving at this point in their travels, delayed by the tardy departure of their more aggressive cousins, the barn swallows, whose nesting range it was.

Without raising his head, Nick Ear brought his big paw to his mouth and began grooming his feet. On a rock some thirty yards away, the old tree bobcat dozed. She would have been undetectable against the dimpled stone had not her tail and paws twitched in her sleep. The old bobcat was dreaming.

To the north, pronghorns were filing into the desert valley. Protected by two mountain chains, the sage plain served as winter range for these animals, known locally as antelope, and had done so for longer than man had walked the continent. In the lead was an alert doe who took high steps, held her head erect, and missed nothing. Her large eyes, conveniently placed on the sides of her head,

provided wide-angle vision. Alongside the flowing animals ran a buck; like a cow pony whose duty it is to keep cattle from scattering, he patrolled the herd.

The young bobcat noticed the faraway animals flowing into the valley. From such a distance, they resembled a crawl of bugs, their pronged horns looking like antennae. For a long time he studied them. Then his pupils narrowed, and once again he focused on the horned lizard directly below him. At last, when the measure of his curiosity began to exceed that of his inertia, he stood up and stretched. Then, in easy leaps, he let himself down from his sunning place.

The horned lizard heard the thud of the cat's four feet meeting the hardpan of the desert floor, and it scurried under a stump of sagebrush. Not quickly enough, however. The cat had kept the reptile in view, and a rubbery paw plucked it from hiding and began to probe its rough back. The cat was gentle, investigative, careful. Something about the appearance of the odd-looking creature informed him to be cautious.

The lizard, in spite of its rough-looking skin, was exquisitely sensitive. A network of nerve endings extended to the tips of its dead-looking scales and provided the animal with subtle information about its surroundings, even registered slight changes in temperature. Now the cat's warm paw pressure told the lizard to mobilize all of its defense tactics. Gasping air, the creature rapidly pumped up its dimensions. Simultaneously, blood surged through its body, building pressure until two membranes in its eye corners burst open and a jet of the vital fluid spewed out.

The bobcat jumped backward. The sudden ejaculation alarmed him, and by the time the bobcat had recovered his composure, the horned lizard was gone. Somewhere nearby, it was playing the old game of "statue," posing like a desert plant. Its daggerlike horns mimicked a calyx of sepals; its relatively small head imitated a bud. The illusion fooled the cat, who passed the trompe l'oeil without discovering the deception.

Chapter 13

The tree bobcat awoke with a start. The sharp retort of gunfire rang in her ears. She lifted her head. On the horizon a puff of dust extruded into a long tail as a herd of antelope sped across the sage. They soared like winged horses over the low brush, a blur of animals moving at sixty miles an hour. On their rumps, white patches of hair stood erect, signaling danger, notifying every antelope within eyeshot to take flight. Beneath these white patches, twin glands released strong, musky scent, which caused another band of antelope a half mile downwind to raise their heads and distend their nostrils. Then they, too, joined in the flight, and in the bright sunlight their heliographic rumps flashed the same white code, a signal seen by even more of their kind. These animals, too, began to stampede.

A pickup truck bounced across the dry land in hot pursuit. Two more loud cracks sounded, and a doe in the lead pitched to the ground. The fleeing animals ran over her.

The herd had traveled two miles in two minutes when it stopped. The antelope looked back at their pursuer. Their incredible speed had purchased them a few minutes' rest. They had outdistanced the truck. No animal in North America could run so fast as they.

Nevertheless, their capacity for bursts of speed was no match for man's technology. They did not possess the stamina of a truck, and even before the vehicle drew near enough to spur them into another headlong dash, the antelope felt the long teeth of bullets snapping at their hoofs, snagging the ground, pelting them with clods of dirt.

Explosively, the herd was set in motion again. Their leaps were

115

prodigious. The animals cleared clumps of desert brush without up-rooting a single plant. They moved as a unit—wheeling, turning, bounding as if directed by a single mind.

The truck bumped clumsily after them, crushing vegetation in its path. Three men inside clung to window frames and dashboards, bracing themselves against the violent jolts. The men were oblivious to the damage their vehicle was causing the fragile terrain. Their lives were removed from those of the creatures sustained by this desert ecosystem. They clutched their rifles.

The truck angled toward the wheeling herd and braked, and more gunfire spewed at the antelope. A yearling doe buckled and dropped to the ground. The pickup started up and once again roared after the fleeing herd. The appetite of its occupants for victims was not yet appeased. The truck contained trophy hunters, who, unlike wild predators, did not quit the chase when an animal was felled.

In times past, when wolves still prowled the Idaho sage, ances-tors of these antelope were sometimes run by relays of the wild can-ids. But those chases had been of short duration, ending when the wolves obtained their objective, a single victim—or sooner if the prospect of hunting success appeared to the wolves to be poor. Wolves had to economize energy; they could not expend hard-earned calories in fruitless pursuits. This kind of predation had benefited the antelope herd. More often than not, the wolves were only able to kill weaklings or misfits, and so they prevented poor specimens from passing their genes on to future generations. The wolves performed this culling service quite inadvertently. They caught what animals they could catch, and great skill and strength and cunning and speed were exacted of them just to bring down a sickly, lame, or unintelligent specimen. Only rarely did a wolf pack succeed in killing a healthy adult antelope of breeding age, one that was genetically and socially valuable to the herd.

By contrast, the men in the truck did not take aim at the poor-est-looking specimens. They were after superior animals, heads to mount. The antelope they wanted possessed the most impressive horns, headgear only worn by the strongest, the survivors. So, un-like wolf predation, the effect of trophy hunting on the herd was the extinction of the best.

That a doe and a yearling had been felled was incidental, unin-tentional, even an embarrassment to the men. Now, to uphold their reputations, they disdained to pick up the evidence, and they pressed on. They wanted only bucks.

Firing on animals from a moving vehicle was illegal in the state of Idaho. But the Department of Fish and Game was understaffed to oversee the state's vast and rugged terrain, and scofflaws ran little risk of being apprehended and fined. Poaching was commonplace, often carried out just for the thrill of defying authority.

To the wild antelope, however, even legitimate, well-regulated sport hunting was stressful. The animals' defenses had evolved over millennia, had been shaped by another kind of reality—one in which predator and prey met on the same difficult ground. This, however, was no longer the case. Now a predator had defected from the natural order. Now a predator pursued them who had equipped his eyes with telephoto lenses, had substituted wheels for his legs, and had extended his reach to the distance a bullet could fly. To regain parity with such an unnatural being was not possible for the antelope, would require eons of evolutionary time. And, at the moment, the panicky herd had only seconds to hurtle out of firing range.

From a natural grandstand, an andesite outcropping, two bobcats watched as the frenzied creatures bounded past, noted the approach of a second pickup truck, saw it head off the herd, honking and roaring. As the antelope were turned into a volley of bullets, the two cats made a dash for a rock crevice, but the squack of walkie-talkies, the roar of strained engines, and the shouts of men followed them into their hiding place.

That no buck had been struck by the barrage of gunfire was in a way unfortunate; the chase would continue until the men had killed what they wanted. So the herd was pressed on. The animals made a wide swing and retraced the same circuitous route past the rock pile. By now the antelopes' tongues were lolling from their mouths like long red ribbons, their sides were heaving, and their panting was punctuated by wheezes and groans. But the men in the trucks gave them no time out. Wolves would have done so, would have required a rest themselves, or else would have given up before reaching such a point of exhaustion. But the trucks were insentient, relentless, and bounced after the animals, burning the kind of energy that cost their passengers no suffering. And the bullets continued to fly.

The cats could not see the bucks give up their lives. They could,

however, hear the men's voices outside their hideout. Like the loud cries of alarmed ravens, the strident sounds aroused fear in the cats, creating physiological changes that readied them to take flight or to stand and fight. But the bobcats were unable to act on either of these impulses, for the proximity of the men compelled them to remain hidden.

Meanwhile, the men, satisfied at last that they had killed animals of impressive dimensions, began to gut their victims. While three of the hunters dressed the carcasses, a fourth took potshots at the nearby rock pile. His act was a casual one. Just as a bobcat obtains relief from the tension of a hunt by playing with a catch, the marksman was working off nervous energy aroused in him by the excitement of the chase. He was unaware of the panic his action was creating inside the mound of stones where the sound of shattering rock was amplified and resonated through every interstice. The bobcats experienced the shock waves as though they were electric jolts. With racing hearts, they cringed and salivated and hunkered down while the hunter repeatedly reloaded and emptied his gun at his improvised target.

At last it was over. Outside, three bucks had been gutted, their bloody offal spread about on the ground. The four men climbed into the trucks and roared off, leaving in their wake a strange silence, a silence that could be heard and felt and seemed to possess a kind of presence, like the eye of a storm. No insect buzzed, no bird piped, no animal scurried; and for a long time afterward, nature's faint sound track of rustle and hum did not resume playing.

But the quietus that hung like a heat wave over the place was not heard by Nick Ear. His head was throbbing with the drumming sound of his own pulse. His sympathetic nervous system was not functioning properly. It had been overstimulated by the terrifying sound of bullets and the proximity of men. Now hormones flooded his body, raising his blood pressure. Sweat oozed from his paw pads, yet he shivered with cold, for his vascular system was also malfunctioning. His third eyelid everted, and when the tree bobcat, against whom he huddled, got to her feet, Nick Ear's body dropped to the floor of the cave and went limp. He was in shock.

That he should react so to fright was no aberrant symptom. The bobcat's nervous system was designed to meet the needs of a solitary, self-reliant being. During the course of his lifetime, he would have to depend solely on his own ears, his own eyes, his own sense

of smell, and, most important, his own high degree of caution, to alert him to danger. For unlike a coyote or an antelope, no pack or herd member would spell him from the necessity of acting as his own sentinel. Therefore, he was keenly aware and excruciatingly sensitive. But being endowed with such a finely tuned automatic nervous system carried with it a high price: it could become overloaded. If the stimuli it processed were too compelling, too persistent, too inescapable, a bobcat could go into shock, even die.

The tree bobcat nudged him, but when even her gentle grooming failed to evoke a response, she left him, climbed out of the rock crevice, and headed for the streambed. In September, the solar day ended early, and now the chill air told her that rabbits would be active.

That night the tree bobcat caught a large jackrabbit. After eating as much as she wanted, she played with what remained. Perhaps the season was past for a mother cat to drag food across entangling vegetation to hungry young. For by now, hungry young were accompanying their mothers, were being taken to rabbits instead of the other way round. Or perhaps the events of the day and Nick Ear's strange behavior had simply faded from the old cat's mind. Whatever her bobcat reason, she did not return to the kitten that night. And the whole of the next day, she remained by the stream and slept under a tent of broken willow stems.

When she awoke, it was dusk. For a long time she remained still, waiting and watching for something to move. At last a twitch in the willows sent her soaring through the air, and she landed on the back of a cottontail. Catching two rabbits in as many days was sheer prosperity, and the food could put the old cat back into condition. But she hardly did more than taste this rabbit. After plucking fur along its back, she suddenly pushed the entire carcass under her body, lion fashion, and gripping it by the neck, began to drag it up the steep cliff.

She knew the shortest ascent route to take, but she chose another, one where the gradient had been modified by a rockslide. Even so, she had difficulty maneuvering the steep climb, and, at one point, she accidentally let go of the rabbit and had to drop back to retrieve it. On her next try she made it all the way to the top with her cargo in tow.

The rest of her trip presented other difficulties. Her progress across the sage plain was repeatedy impeded when the rabbit she dragged became snagged on vegetation. At last, however, she arrived at her destination, where, exhausted, she dropped her burden and called. The contented sound she produced was intended to announce to her kitten that she had brought a rabbit, but her satisfied chortle called forth no response from inside the rock cavity. Nick Ear, if he heard the old cat's chirrup, merely incorporated the sound into his dream. The tree bobcat repeated her call. Finally, when no kitten came bounding out to receive her offering, she began to eat it herself. She was hungry, and devoured the raw meat in convulsive swallows. From time to time she had to cough up an oversized bite, too hastily consumed, and eat it a second time.

Inside the cave, the kitten was waking up, and, gradually, he began to register the sound of crunching bones. After a while he got to his feet, wobbled over to the rock opening, and peered out. Below him, in the dim light, he could make out the outline of a feeding

bobcat, and as the vision took shape in his brain, the act of focusing and registering a perception was therapeutic to the ailing kitten. For some time he sat quietly and continued to watch the tree bobcat eat.

The tree bobcat, when she became aware that she was being observed, growled and repositioned herself to shield her meal from the kitten's view. Having now tasted it, the old cat no longer felt any inclination to share this rabbit. Satisfying her own appetite was all that interested her. The old bobcat's change of heart mattered little to Nick Ear. The food that he now craved was not rabbit. His nervous system was gradually restoring connections and needed input. He responded to events around him like a person who is coming out of anesthesia; he struggled to bring his surroundings into focus.

When the tree bobcat finished eating, she batted the rabbit's remains, which flew high in the air. Nick Ear tracked their path with his eyes and noted where they landed. When the tree bobcat, uncharacteristically, scraped dirt over the carcass, this, too, he registered. At a later date he would imitate the behavior. Nick Ear had recovered.

That night the tree bobcat and her foster kitten twined together and slept. Though the season was near at hand when mother bobcats would begin to withdraw support from their young, the tree bobcat was not of a mind to abandon Nick Ear.

Chapter 14

By late fall most of the animals in the northwest had prepared for winter. The voles and the white-footed mice and the prairie dogs had responded to the gradual shortening of daylight by becoming hyperactive, scurrying about and storing provisions against the lean season ahead. Diminishing light had the opposite effect on chipmunks and spotted bats. It slowed their metabolic rate, readying them for a period of hibernation.

The bobcats experienced no such change. Though reduced exposure to daylight did cause their coats to grow longer and thicker, it produced in them neither a show of providence nor signs of lethargy. Their diet of meat was not one that could be easily warehoused, like seeds or nuts. At the same time, nature had neglected to program the bobcat to sleep through the months of bitter cold,

when prey species would be in short supply. As a result, the oncoming season would prey on the bobcat population as unsparingly as the bobcat itself hunted animals positioned below it on the food chain. Only the most vital individuals would escape winter's rigors.

Yet, in the long run, arctic weather would benefit the bobcat. Winter was a leveler that kept a species viable, a predator that preyed on predators. The eagle, the fox, the weasel, the coyote—all these flesh eaters experienced an annual die-off that, paradoxically, insured their long-range survival by eliminating the unfit.

That these populations of predatory animals be held in check was of critical importance. For should one of the meat eaters come to outnumber the prey species it consumed, it would eat up its food supply and cause the extinction of the species that fed it; inevitably, its own extinction would ensue. The fact that no such calamity had befallen any present-day predators—all of which had survived eons of evolutionary history—was proof that nature's mechanisms to depress these populations had been fail-safe. Winter was of course only one of these limiting factors: drought, prey cycles, crowding, and disease also held predators to numbers compatible with their food supply. Winter, however, was an inexorable force, a most reliable depredator. Individually, animals who stood high on the food chain did not survive many of these annual purges.

Yet the tree bobcat had lived through fifteen—a feat that testified to her individual superiority. Now, however, as cold weather approached, she did not look well. Beneath her matted coat, her bony frame pressed against shrunken skin. Her hind legs were stiff, and one of her canine teeth had recently broken off. Yet, in spite of physical deterioration, her spirit remained that of a young cat, and she continued to indulge her foundling kitten as if she were a new mother.

Now that Nick Ear had fully recovered from his siege of shock, he faced each day with blithe indifference to the future. Though he lacked a sibling with whom to romp, his delight in play did not diminish. Sometimes he succeeded in enticing the old tree bobcat to join in one of his wild games, to assume the role of pursuer or pursuee. At other times, he chased and leaped upon phantom playmates or ambushed the loose tumbleweed that bowled about the desert at high speed.

Nick Ear was developing rapidly, losing his kittenish appearance and acquiring the lanky look of an adolescent. Still, at six months, he had not yet gained the weight he would attain at maturity. Nor had his testicles descended; they would not appear for another five months, and more than two years would have to pass before his hormonal output would reach a level sufficient for him to father kittens of his own. Like all intelligent species, his physical development was slow, his adolescent period of dependency long. Lacking a complete set of stereotypical responses to life situations, he had to learn how to meet the exigencies of living one by one. And learning took time.

One day, en route to the stream, he and his surrogate mother caught sight of a strange bobcat. The animal, a lean tom, was approaching upwind and so failed to hear or smell the two of them. With elegant patience, they waited, studying the approaching trespasser with unblinking attentiveness. As the tom drew nearer, Nick Ear made a sprint in his direction and would have revealed himself to the intruder had not a quiet growl from the tree bobcat stopped him. Her rebuke set him back on his haunches, and even evoked from him a yawn, a signal of his sudden lack of interest in pursuing the course of action she found objectionable.

Meanwhile, the lean bobcat continued to approach along the path that would inevitably bring him face to face with the resident cats. But the tree bobcat was in no mood for an encounter and stealthily withdrew into brush. Nick Ear, of course, followed, and from a hidden vantage point, an outcropping of lava, the two cats watched as the transient animal moved along one of their own well-traveled routes.

In a showdown with this stranger, the tree bobcat would almost certainly be victorious, simply by virtue of the high level of confidence that residency engenders in wild animals. Nevertheless, she preferred to avoid combat. When the tomcat had passed from view, she and Nick Ear quit their hiding place and headed in the opposite direction from the one he had taken. The incident was closed.

But the tree bobcat's act of withdrawal in no way signified concession on her part. Her claim to the range she occupied was simply not threatened by the visit of a stranger. She would preserve her tenure, and without the need to resort to aggressive action. Her scent markings, liberally scattered throughout the area, were adequate repellents to drive away strangers. The lean tom, no less than the tree bobcat, shared the species' distaste for contact with kind, and he soon would depart the area without needing to be routed.

Even so, during her long lifetime, the tree bobcat had not always been able to avoid combat. On a few occasions, when a surprise encounter had foreclosed the option of withdrawal, she had attacked an invader. Moreover, during the first weeks following the birth of a litter, her mood was invariably contentious, and she sometimes sought out adversaries along the borders of her home range just to rout them. But this maternal belligerence was transitory and hormonally induced, much like the heightened aggressiveness of males during the mating season.

In most circumstances the bobcat's innate aloofness saved her from having to do battle. Equipped as she was with fangs and claws that could kill, some such deterrent was necessary, had had to evolve to prevent the species from doing itself harm.

Wild canids had devised quite a different solution to the danger of their own aggressivity. Wolves could not practice avoidance behavior. They had to coexist in packs, requiring, as they did, one another's assistance to bring down large prey. Wolves, therefore, had evolved social strategies to help them maintain harmony. In each

pack a hierarchy was formed and respected. Should any two members contend over a choice piece of meat, the subordinate wolf would automatically concede it to the more dominant one. And the animal showing deference would prostrate himself, thus defusing the aggressivity he had aroused in the stronger animal. Afterward, friendly relations would be restored and reinforced through group howls, or by tail wagging and face licking.

But if the canids invented sociability, the felids authored aloofness, and, paradoxically, the two families' dissimilar life-styles sprang from the same need to guard against self-destruction. Yet, though the old tree bobcat now headed in the opposite direction from that taken by the lean tomcat, she could not avoid coming upon the scat piles the stranger had left behind, an inspection of which provided her with some information about the animal. Pheromones in his waste told her the sex of the trespasser, and undigested food particles indicated that he had recently been feeding on fish.

Nick Ear watched as the tree bobcat covered this alien sign with her own spray and set about re-marking her regular travel routes. But the odor of urine was ephemeral and would dissipate in a few days. A conspicuous pile of uncovered fecal matter, on the other hand, would leave a more lasting message. The old cat posted a pathway with a pile of stools and underscored the fetid communiqué with visible claw scrapings on the ground. Possibly to deposit several such notices of her current status, she remained in the area over the next few days, and, during that time, she succeeded in producing a remarkable number of stools. Meanwhile, to feed herself and Nick Ear, she visited the stream each night and fished.

The male cutthroat trout were by now exhibiting flashy spawning colors, and the females were ripe with vitamin-rich eggs. Their stomachs were full of the larvae of caddis flies, stone flies, and mayflies, important particles of biomass which would move up through the food chain according to an intricate design that did not demand understanding on the part of the pyramid of animals being served. To the old bobcat, who relished trout, insects were merely a nuisance. The part they played in her own survival was knowledge she would never possess. She simply harvested the fish they nourished and relished the diet.

Nick Ear, too, eagerly devoured the trout the tree bobcat caught for him, ate the scales, bones, and all, and was none the worse for

it. In addition, he enjoyed playing with the lively quarry, pouncing and sliding on the gasping victims that his guardian skillfully batted onto shore. When a fish managed to flop its way back to its proper element, he would splash in after it, unmindful of the sensation of wetness. His earlier experience in water, harrowing as it had been, had apparently faded from his memory.

One day he, too, began to fish. He failed to make a catch, but his effort to do so was in itself an achievement. Once it had occurred to him that he could obtain this food for himself, it did not take him long to acquire the skill to do so. A few hours of practice perfected those moves that proved successful and eliminated those that were counterproductive. In the end, his technique for snaring slippery prey was uniquely his.

Although self-taught, the kitten would probably not have acquired this skill if he had not first observed the tree bobcat's success at it. The young bobcat's ability to gain information by observing the actions of another was as important as instinct, as important as learning by trial and error. To exploit this capacity for imitation, nature had granted young bobcats a long association with their mothers. A mother bobcat, while performing any number of obvious services for her young, licking their wounds, bringing them food, cautioning, grooming, and guarding them, quite unintentionally acted as a role model. And this inadvertent service was of no less importance to the development of her young than all her purposeful labor.

Nick Ear's period of dependency was preordained, and while his attachment to the tree bobcat was undoubtedly gratifying to her, even this bond would be dissolved in due course. In a few months' time, the same female cat who now shared her food with this kitten would no longer tolerate his presence. In February or March, when the urge to mate would again come upon her, she would reject Nick Ear. And the cold season, cruel to all animals, would make no special allowances for a young bobcat trying to make his own way for the first time. Winter would be uncompromising. Winter would be a dispassionate slayer. Winter was always a perilous time for the very old and the very young.

Chapter 15

The sky had been winnowing snow since early morning, but though the air danced with the white siftings, the desert remained uncovered. Only here and there did wet crystals settle on vegetation or streak rocks. Most of the snow evaporated on contact with the warmer ground.

Still, the swirling, cold flakes excited Nick Ear. Like some humless horde of insects, they bit his nose, causing him to swat back in self-defense. There was sport to be made from such weather. The air was alive, visible, moving. Yet the dancing whorls mysteriously melted to nothingness on a bobcat's tongue and fur. Nick Ear pranced.

The tree bobcat growled a warning at the rambunctious adolescent and took shelter under a rock overhang. She had seen all this happen before. If the first snowfall of the year failed to revive in her cat brain memories of past hardships, it certainly did not bring her any pleasure. Her bones, barometers of seasonal change, ached.

But the tree bobcat's reprimand had no effect on Nick Ear. He could not be subdued. He leaped about the cliff face, skidding across wet boulders. He soared from rock pinnacle to rock pinnacle, making and breaking new records for his longest jump. He chased and escaped from aerial apparitions visible only to kittens. No fear inhibited the cat. He executed his daring jumps as if he were indestructible. The chasms beneath him existed only to be defied; the space before him existed only to be experienced. Nick Ear's confidence soared higher than his leaps.

But then he miscalculated. He overshot a mark. With claws scraping across slick rock, he failed to brake and somersaulted off a thirty-foot drop. For a fraction of a second he fell face-up, while vestibular organs in his ears screamed signals for him to right himself. With violent effort he wrenched his shoulders round, twisting hard against the resistance of the still-upturned rear half of his body. This he managed while falling, falling like a meteorite, plummeting without wings to beat against the awesome suck of gravity, without membranes to spread like braking sails.

But the cat was a coiled spring. Before striking earth, the hind part of his torso spiraled round. Four paws touched ground simultaneously to absorb the shock of impact. This extraordinary rotary flip, executed in just one-eighth of a second, saved his life. Of the higher animals, only the felines could perform such prodigious feats.

For several minutes afterward, Nick Ear remained motionless. His legs weren't broken, yet stabs of pain surged through them. The exertion of righting himself midair, then locking his muscles to prevent further spin, had demanded all his available energy. He sat hunched, awaiting recovery.

The tree bobcat had not seen Nick Ear catapult over the cliff-side. She lay huddled under a rock, eyes closed, forepaws neatly tucked into her long chest hair. Her whole attention was centered on her own physical state. So self-absorbed was she that she didn't even notice Nick Ear's absence. Snow was beginning to stick to rocks and brush, and the tree bobcat made herself small to conserve warmth and keep dry. She had not survived fifteen winters by allowing precious calories to escape into the vast heat sink that was an Idaho winter sky.

When the throbbing in Nick Ear's paws subsided, he tried to rise, but his legs quivered. Coordinates of large and small muscle groups, those which enabled him to walk narrow spans—tree branches and rock ledges—were responding erratically to signals being sent by his brain. With uneven gait he made his way to an alcove at the base of the rock wall, there to hole up. He would not attempt to climb back up the cliff face that day.

All night, while Nick Ear remained still, the air oscillated with snow and the temperature plummeted. And during the whole of the next day no animal moved, as a low sky continued to sift its heavy contents onto the desert floor, filling the canyon trench with drifts and whiting out the surrounding mountains. Every wild creature's world shrank to the small circle of space that remained visible before it. Beings were isolated, their movements restricted. All life was forced into submissiveness by an indifferent nature.

Nick Ear longed to curl up with the tree bobcat, to nestle in her musky fur. The kitten in him was still a social animal, yet he was already better able to bear isolation than were the truly gregarious species, the wild canids and the herd animals. Being a male cat, he was destined to mature into a recluse, a creature who would walk by himself.

For the present, he took comfort in the security provided by his snug rock shelter. It protected him from the wind and the snow. His soft undercoat, as lightweight and efficient as wild goose down, further insulated him against the bitter cold. Long, gleaming guard hairs, individually pigmented with bands of pale gold and gray, covered this soft underfur and waterproofed it. And a magnificent bib of creamy white hair, flecked with black, hung from his chest and belly.

It was precisely this piece of the bobcat's winter pelt that at that very moment was inciting trappers to make plans to visit the

high desert. Just this small piece of spotted fur commanded big money on the fur market. Trapping season was about to open, and, while the coats of the coyote, the badger, the fox, and the otter had all increased in value, it was the bobcat's belly the men most wanted. A single one could pay for a new Honda. Throughout the state, snowmobiles were being tanked up, traplines made ready, scent lures concocted, and unconcealed excitement could be heard in men's voices as they exchanged information about the "season" and "tracks" and "dealer prices."

In times past, trapping had been the province of a few old-timers in need of supplemental income. Lately, however, wild fur had become the fashion rage, and everybody wanted to get in on it. Retired people, schoolteachers, gas-station attendants, ranch wives, even children set traplines; and the gory business was now being called a sport. Wildlife managers in every state set new, higher prices on the trapping licenses they sold, and they welcomed the increase in revenue.

It was not for warmth that bobcat coats had suddenly come into vogue, nor was it because the fur was especially durable. It wasn't. Bobcat fur shed on furniture and skirts and could not be guaranteed to give three seasons' wear. What had created the inflated price was the near extinction of cheetahs and leopards and other species of spotted cats. Bobcat pelts were substituted. Eleven belly skins pieced together and dignified with the name "lynx cat" could be fashioned into a stylish coat that would market for several thousand dollars. Such a coat might cost the Idaho wilderness every bobcat inhabiting a hundred square miles. "Lynx cat" was indeed a luxury item.

That the bobcat had evolved this coveted belly hair to insure its survival, to shield its vital organs from direct contact with snow, was a supreme irony. That biological advantage, created over millennia of natural selection, was suddenly the very feature that marked the animal for rapid and unnatural decline. Once again the aims of natural selection and human exploitation were mutually exclusive.

Late in the afternoon, the storm ended, and Nick Ear knew that rodents would be out. Even in cave gloom, his time sense was unerring, bound to his circadian rhythms, nudged by stomach contractions, and in tune with his ever-recurring need to discharge predatory energy. The young bobcat raised up, but his movements did not feel fluid and pleasurable, as a cat's should. One by one he flexed each of his four legs. Then he gave both of his front paws a vigorous shake. Next he washed his shoulders and back. The firm stroking action of a warm tongue brought relief to tight places, places only indirectly connected with the musculature being massaged. When he finished grooming himself, his coordination had improved and he walked with steady gait to the door of the alcove.

Outside, snow was heaped along the stream bank, altering the contours of the setting so that he no longer knew the place. Every bush was obliterated, every rock pile buried from view. The dazzling expanse shuttered down his pupils until his amber irises almost filled his eye sockets. He gazed, dumbstruck.

A horned lark, skittering about on the white glaze, caught his attention. The lark did not hop like most birds, but walked, chicken-fashion, one foot in front of the other. Its evenly spaced toeprints might have been designs etched on a cake, so neatly were the flourishes laid down.

Already, beneath the gleaming pack, between the ground surface and the snow dome, voles were busy creating tunnels. Inside their communal works, they would remain awake and active until a spring thaw melted their crystal roof, offering them up to hungry bobcats and owls and the pair of rough-legged hawks who wintered on the high plain. Even now, they were not safe from the more enterprising predators, the coyotes and the weasels. A coyote could nose-dive into their snow towns to seize any noisy individual who unwittingly betrayed his precise location. And weasels would not hesitate to tunnel into the snowy mazes to surprise and kill the little rodents inside their own winter quarters. Yet, despite these ongoing losses, the voles' adaptation to the small-scale glacial epoch that was upon them was a good one. It guaranteed the survival of a viable number of the species.

Even now, as the little, grizzled workers were busily plugging up all the entryways to their subnivean chambers, a long-tailed weasel was nosing about overhead, tunneling through soft drifts like some kind of miniature but high-powered snow-moving machine. The storm had interfered with the lithe creature's feeding schedule, and hunger was driving it to hunt at a frenetic pace. Its rapid metabolism—a body temperature of 105 degrees and 421 heartbeats per minute—had consigned the animal to live its life at an accelerated pace.

Perhaps the weasel's own subjective experience of its hyperactive existence was no different from that of a sluggish turtle alloted a century of time in the sun. Nevertheless, the animal, geared as it was to a different time frame, suffered certain handicaps; for, in a world of creatures in tune with the planetary day, the weasel's relentless food demands did not always coincide with the routines of available prey. Nor could it postpone hunting, even when weather conditions sent every potential victim under cover. The weasel had to follow, dive into burrow or warren, slip into coop or culvert. A bobcat or a coyote could wait out a storm, could survive a fast lasting many days. A weasel, come what may, had to feed every few hours just to sustain its accelerated existence.

And so, even before the storm had subsided, the feisty predator was out seeking food, and its undulating movements, as it nosed about on fragile snow crust, excited the bobcat. Its light brown body, here and there blotched with white, appeared to be in molt. In actual fact, the weasel was dressing up for winter, suiting itself in royal ermine, a display of glory that would put the elongated mustelid's very life in jeopardy; for in its all-white phase the animal brought a better price at the winter fur auctions. As with the bobcat's long belly fur, the natural advantage offered the weasel by a seasonal change of dress was an adaptation that now imperiled its continued existence.

Nick Ear tested the snow with a forefoot. The sensation of cold quickly brought his paw pad to his tongue. Assiduously, he licked snow crystals from between his toes. For the present, his impulse to venture out into the transformed world was checked, and he withdrew a few inches into the cave, seating himself so he faced the shelter opening. For the time being, he would have to content himself with being an onlooker.

He enjoyed hiding. He obtained satisfaction from keeping his presence a secret from the creatures he watched. He was sufficiently self-controlled to remain inactive for extended periods of time. He experienced no compulsion to rush outside and act upon the strangely altered environment, to hoard food or make a nest. Like all wild felines, he lived in the certainty of every transient moment.

For hours he sat placidly and observed what few intrepid animals were foraging in the new snow. He watched the weasel as it nosed its way to the surface of a drift and scrubbed telltale blood traces from its face. He listened to the alarm cries of larks, as they

notified one another of the lurking presence of a predatory bird—an owl or a hawk, perhaps. At times he sat with eyes unfocused, experiencing his own life flow. Being alive was good, sufficient, all that mattered. In his attachment to existence, he was kin to every sentient being. He lived to serve his own self-interests, even as he inadvertently was serving a larger order, a web of matter indescribably intricate.

Hours passed, yet Nick Ear did not grow restive, nor did his watchfulness flag. In his ability to sustain a dichotomous state of physical stillness and mental alertness, he was the equal of spiders and lizards. Like them, he could lie in wait for indeterminate periods in the expectation that the random movements of prey would eventually put some victim within his grasp. The strategy was not ineffective, although most predatory species—the coyote, the fox, the weasel, the fisher—possessed noses too sensitive to try it. One whiff of prey compelled these scent hunters to follow fresh tracks as if pulled along by a nose ring.

That is not to say that the young bobcat did not also move about and hunt in calculated fashion. He did. A keen nose, however, did not distract him in situations calling for patience and attentiveness. Like others of his kind, he rarely applied his sense of smell to the task of hunting, but used it to process other kinds of information—to check on hormone levels in urine splashes left by fellow bobcats, to decipher pheromone messages his neighbors released on the wind, to drink in the euphoric exudate of wild thyme and catnip. To locate and stalk prey, he relied primarily on his ears and his eyes.

He could hear a rustle or a squeak a hundred yards away and creep within pouncing distance of it without disclosing his presence. In thick and crackly vegetation, this was no mean trick. Where dense cover obscured his vision, he hunted entirely by ear, taking repeated sound readings of his intended victim's shifting position while quietly maneuvering into striking range. Often the rustle or thud he so precisely located would turn out in the end to be made by an inedible creature. Hunting by ear demanded not only patience and single-mindedness but a high tolerance for failure. A bobcat is not short on any of these traits.

Nick Ear's incredible ability to pick up mere whispers of sound explained how he knew it when a winterized jackrabbit popped from a snow warren near his place of shelter. The animal could not have been more efficiently camouflaged, its white coat a blank against the snowy backdrop. Though its hard feet met the powdery drifts in soundless rotation, the creature was doomed. Nick Ear had heard it grind its teeth.

No longer did the prospect of snow sticking to his feet give him pause. Electrified, he sank into a preparatory crouch, his hind legs treading, his tail twitching. His entire being was charged with predatory energy.

The white-tailed jackrabbit was careless. It hopped about, kicking up snow sprays, and neglected to be vigilant. It never saw the bobcat, received no warning of impending ambush. Its brain held but a single thought—willow bark. When the cat sprang, the rabbit was heading toward the stream bank where that staple was swaying in tinkling and icy profusion. One scream, muted by snow and amplified by ancient rock, announced that the violent deed was done. It was a protest without purpose. Rabbits are never rescued by the universe they cry out to. Even while air was still passing through its larynx, the animal gave up its life.

Nick Ear cleaned his paws and face, then dragged the warm corpse back to his lair, where he could feast in private. The mere scent of the animal transported him, sent him into such a rapture that, before settling down to feast, he rolled and rubbed against the creature's furry remains in a kind of euphoric celebration. Though he had killed only one other rabbit in his lifetime, he knew that no better food existed. He had enjoyed enough of the tree bobcat's catches to be convinced of that.

But now some time had elapsed since he had tasted this preferred food. For several weeks the tree bobcat had warned him away from her kills, giving ferocious notice that, so far as this kind of meat was concerned, Nick Ear was no longer on the dole; if he wished to indulge his taste for rabbit, he would have to catch his own.

So, for the second time, he had done just that. His first victim had been only a small cottontail. Now, however, he had succeeded in securing for himself a full-grown jackrabbit—ten pounds of meat! The bobcat growled as he tore into the animal's hide and chattered as he chewed through its neck and severed its head. Nick Ear's aggression was not directed at anything in particular, but was meant only to discourage any animal within earshot from making a raid on his prize. For too long he had subsisted on deer mice and chipmunks and kangaroo rats and voles. Now he would not be dispossessed of a rabbit, however formidable might be his challenger. Young though he was, Nick Ear was already enough of a bobcat to make a fearless stand over such a bonanza.

He could not hope to consume the entire carcass at one feeding, but he tried. He ate until his belly bulged and was hard. He ate until he hurt. He ate until he could scarcely move.

It was a fine way to begin winter. In one swift act, the young bobcat had provided himself with the most perfect food nature had devised for him. He had also satisfied one of his deepest, most primal urges. He was born to be a master hunter of rabbits.

WINTER

Chapter 16

The bobcats were restricted by snow, their movements limited to a few maneuverable sites. They clung to cliff walls, bivouacked in caves, and hunted on windswept rises. When forced to walk on the treacherous stuff, they took tentative steps, for they lacked the snowshoe feet of their cousin, the Canada lynx, and when they broke through, they paid dearly to extricate themselves. In cold weather, a bobcat could ill afford to spend precious reserves leaping and swimming out of heavy drifts to the haven of a protruding rock or log.

Nick Ear followed the example of the tree bobcat and quickly learned to take advantage of trails plowed out by mule deer and elk and afterward trampled hard by the many animals who made use of them. But many of these trenches did not lead in promising directions, and traveling them was not without hazard. Strange cats or hungry coyotes could appear unexpectedly from around any blind curve, and a head-on meeting in a snow furrow was almost certain to end in bloodshed. Without tree or rock pile at hand, escape was not a feasible option.

Jackrabbit runways were safer, more elevated, and provided better visibility. These thoroughfares of pounded snow were surprisingly firm, strong enough to support a man's weight. Though in early winter they led only from warren entryway to the nearest protruding bush, as the season progressed and uneaten sage tips became progressively more distant, rabbit runways grew more extensive and became serviceable travel routes for bobcats.

Bobcats put them to another use, too: they concealed themselves in the soft snow that mounded on either side of a rabbit trail and waited there to ambush the little roadmakers as they hopped

past. In so doing, they demonstrated their capacity for laying plans, showed themselves to be more than merely opportunistic in their approach to food finding.

Nick Ear's ability to bring down prey was developing. He watched the tree bobcat bury herself in drifts alongside rabbit trails and, after taking note of the outcome of this ploy, added the trick to his own repertoire. It was not without purpose that nature had forged the mother-kitten bond to survive well into winter. Each season presented unique challenges to inexperienced young bobcats.

Sometimes, on bright days, the heat of the sun would melt the surface of the white snowscape, creating a thin layer of liquid that would refreeze at sundown to form a hard crust. When this happened, young Nick Ear scampered about on top of the glaze and spent a moon-illuminated night chasing silver prey. In the morning, however, he had to be quick to find hard pack before the sun turned his pleasure arena into a mire.

Increasingly now, the tree bobcat withheld food from Nick Ear. During this season of want, dividing too little could spell starvation for both cats. It was, therefore, in the best interest of the species that the more capable animal, the female of breeding age, should begin to act in a self-serving manner. As early as December, across the northwest, bobcat mothers were growing deaf to the importunate cries of their half-grown young and, in their very presence, were consuming whole pack rats, birds, and entire cottontails. A jackrabbit carcass, however, was usually still being shared, for ten pounds of meat and bone was more food than even a ravenous bobcat wanted to eat at one feeding. As a consequence, during winters when jackrabbits abounded, a greater number of young bobcats survived.

Four weeks had passed since the tree bobcat had brought down a jackrabbit. Nick Ear had been present on that occasion and watched her do it. For two long minutes the hapless victim had kicked and struggled while the old bobcat maintained a relentless grip on its neck. When at last it convulsed and died, she let it drop and appeared to be in no hurry to make a meal of her prize. In fact, she took a short walk, wandering about on the firm snow until all the nervous excitement she had generated while making the kill was dissipated. Not until she regained her calm did she return, and even then she did not immediately tear into the carcass. First she dragged it to a more agreeable feeding site. Then she cleaned herself.

Nick Ear observed this ritual with concealed interest, yet he made no move to confiscate the rabbit. Though he was very hungry, he was not so uninitiated as to assume that the tree bobcat's apparent indifference to her kill meant that she would relinquish it. Had he shown even a modicum of interest in it, she would have chased him off. The kitten's best hope of garnering some part of her leavings lay in not offending the old cat, while still managing to maintain his presence in the immediate area. He knew how to conduct himself to accomplish this objective: he turned his back and averted his gaze.

When the tree bobcat's excitement had at last subsided, she hunched over the carcass and began energetically plucking fur until the fluff around her head looked as if a milkweed plant had just exploded. Her hunger was as terrible as Nick Ear's; her stomach felt as if a constrictor snake had gripped it. When she had opened a hole in the rabbit's thick hide, she tore out meat and swallowed it in unchewed hunks. Yet she did not consume more food than she needed. As soon as her appetite was appeased, she moved away, leaving a sizable portion of the carcass on the ground. Nick Ear, too, would eat.

The moment the old cat turned her back, the kitten sprang to the leavings. While she cleaned her blood-smeared paws and face, he attacked the raw meat. By some cryptic signal, she had given him permission to do so. Between the two of them, the bobcats managed to consume every edible part of the rabbit before the carcass had time to freeze. Only the creature's head, paws, and stomach did they leave untouched, and, at a later date, jogged by hunger, they would reexamine even these icy remains to see what might be gleaned from them. What little satisfaction they could derive from gnawing on such frozen refuse, however, was likely to be more tactile than nourishing.

It was a brutal winter. Snow piled on snow. Old men likened the weather to conditions they recalled early in the century. Students of climate speculated on the possibility of a worldwide cooling trend. Ranchers, whose cattle were having difficulty rooting down through the deep drifts to eat cured grass, worried that they had not laid in sufficient supplemental feed to last the season. There were

even some who expressed a suspicion that the government, by tampering with the upper atmosphere, had inadvertently altered the climate. Only wild animals accepted the hardships winter dealt them with unquestioning minds. A seasonal cycle of hunger, suffering, and death was their annual and inexorable lot.

Nick Ear and the tree bobcat moved to the streambed, where steep canyon walls afforded some protection from the harsh weather; they took up residency on the perpendicular faces of craggy bluffs, clinging to narrow ledges blown free of snow by wind and gravity. Life on a wall presented no particular hazard to the surefooted cats. Nor were they the only animals to take refuge in a vertical world. Bats and birds and pack rats, too, occupied niches and crevices all along the escarpment, and these creatures now provided food for the bobcats.

One cave, midway up the cliff face, had served as a hibernaculum for generations of little brown bats, and the old cat knew of it. So, when a ledge route to the place was blown free of snow and became passable, she and Nick Ear paid a call on the dormant residents. Inside the grotto, the temperature remained at slightly above freezing, and it was this peculiar stability of temperature that made the cave habitable for wintering bats. If the air were to cool but a few degrees and drop to the freezing point, water in the cells of the torpid bats would escape and the animals would die; on the other hand, should it warm a little, the bats' metabolic rate would increase and burn up all their fat reserves, resulting in their starvation.

As Nick Ear entered the cave, a pungent odor rising from the guano-covered floor excited him even before he noticed the fur-draped ceiling. The tree bobcat, however, was single-minded in her pursuit of food and knew exactly where to look for it. Massive numbers of bats, each one hanging by its thumb hooks, covered every inch of overhead rock.

The hibernating creatures appeared lifeless, drawing only a single breath every five minutes. The animals, in fact, approached as near to death as is possible without succumbing to its finality. Such functions as feeding, digestion, cell replacement, elimination—all had been suspended. Nevertheless, if disturbed, the entire colony was capable of making a rapid resurrection, and, from one hard experience, the tree bobcat knew this. Therefore, when she plucked a victim from the ceiling, she ate it quickly, headfirst, before it had time

150

to sound the alarm which would awaken the entire colony.

Nick Ear, however, was an inexperienced, half-grown kitten, and though he was hungry, his need to release catch-and-toss energy was also pressing—as imperative, in fact, as were the demands of his stomach. He, too, wasted no time pulling down a bat, but, unlike the tree bobcat, he did not take the precaution of biting off his victim's head. Instead, he pitched the creature high in the air.

The sensation of being swatted about revived the little mammal from its winter's nap, and, in no time, it began to protest its rude awakening. Its rapid squeaks in no way resembled the supersonic vocalizations used by bats to avoid collison. The sounds it emitted were in a low frequency, entirely audible, even to a cat, and every sleeping member of the colony was responsive to it.

Nick Ear, of course, did not perceive the significance of the bat's communiqué. Its agitated piping merely served to increase his own pleasure and excitement in bat tossing. When one furry creature slipped his grasp and fluttered upward, he reached for another and then again another, and he failed to observe that the fur-matted rafters over his head were beginning to undulate. Every bat in the cave was coming to life.

The tree bobcat saw what was happening and flattened to the ground in terror. But Nick Ear remained unmindful of the overhead flutter and continued to toss his captives until, suddenly, the entire colony erupted, thousands strong, and the cave became a churning sea of darting, flitting, swooping little brown bats.

The thick suspension of animals blotted out what dim light had penetrated the cave, as uncountable numbers of wings fanned fetid air in the cats' faces. The squeaking deranged their mental processes, and the overhead commotion struck primal terror in them. They flattened their ears and drew in their heads, and neither struck out with paw or fang. It was not that either bobcat lacked fighting spirit. Overhead shadows simply paralyzed them, rendering them powerless. And so, cowering, they waited, waited for a break in the nerve-shattering oscillation, a pause or a space through which they might dart.

The panicked bats also reacted in a way that was not in their own best interest. A few began to vacate the temperature-stable dormitory, blindly heading for places unknown. At first, only a dozen departed. Then, suddenly, as if blown by a whirlwind, the entire colony swept from the cave and swooped across the winter sky like some dark cyclone cloud seeking a place to touch down. The bats' exodus was in all likelihood a death flight, for the probability was poor that the animals would happen upon another suitable hibernaculum in which to sleep through the remainder of the winter.

After their departure, stillness seemed to resound in the cave, and the abrupt cessation of noise was as disquieting to the bobcats as the loud shrieks had been nerve-racking. Now the cats could hear their own rapid breathing, could feel their own beating hearts. For several minutes they remained crouched, unable to move their legs, unable to activate their wills. Then, suddenly, the tree bobcat came to life, bounded for the escarpment ledge, and ran the length of it without a pause. Seconds later, Nick Ear, following her example, streaked out of the cave and along the same precarious shelf.

Even after so unpleasant an episode, the tree bobcat and Nick Ear could not refuse to take risks. Life asked much of the predators, demanded of them courage and a willingness to take action. For these meat eaters, obtaining every meal was a challenge and often dangerous. At the same time, they had to know when not to push their luck. They could not afford to squander energy, nor chance injury, chasing after hopeless objectives. Usually the bobcats tested a situation before launching an all-out attack. Those that appeared unpromising or too hazardous, they would pass up, however great their hunger.

That the bat raid had ended so dismally was not the result of miscalculation on the part of the tree bobcat. She knew perfectly well how to snare a sleeping bat. As on many of her hunting forays, it was the inexperienced kitten who had handicapped her, had foiled her plans. His impulsive behavior had cost both cats much in nervous energy and, worse, had prevented either of them from obtaining the meal they sought. The three bats that the tree bobcat had managed to consume before pandemonium broke loose had added up to no more than a single ounce, the equivalent of one white-footed mouse. The apparent bulk of *Myotis lucifugus* was illusory; thin, membranous wings, stretched between delicate, lightweight finger bones, constituted most of the animal's size. Unless killed and eaten in large quantities, the little brown bat was not an energy-efficient food.

The following day, a midwinter thaw turned the snow to slush and melted an ice sheet that had spanned the stream, but the unseasonably warm weather did not make life easier for the bobcats. Now slush, rather than deep powder, confined the pair to cliff walls, and the icicles that formed between their toes were an added impediment to their mobility. Not until a cold front swept across the high desert and turned the watery snow to granule were the two at last liberated.

Down they descended from their vertical abode. After such a long confinement, their newfound mobility was reason for revelry. They leaped and played on the hard snow crust and soon experienced a restless urge to be on their way. In winter, when prey reproduced slowly, if at all, those predators who would eat responded to inner promptings that directed them to travel.

Off the bobcats set across the flats, stepping with delicate tread atop crisp crust. A mile from the streambed, they arrived at their destination—a lava cave. The roof of this underground cavern was level with the ground, overgrown with brush, and now sported a topping of snow. Its entryway was a concealed cinder cone. Had the old bobcat not possessed prior knowledge of this hidden place, she would not have discovered it in winter.

Inside the cave, a roomy antechamber opened onto numerous

smaller cavities, honeycombs of hiding places to delight a young bobcat. The many niches and tunnels had been formed by venting gases at a time when ancient rivers of rock had poured and incandesced and rocketed orange fireworks that had lit up a year of skies. That planetary outburst, once so formidable a reality, seemed in the snow-blanketed present to be the improbable conjecture of a mad scientist. Now stillness seemed the only verity.

The lava cave served the bobcats well. During most of every day they remained underground, for the dazzling white snow pained their eyes and made them squint. On cloudy afternoons, however, they sometimes surfaced before the sun dropped behind the surrounding mountains, when pygmy rabbits emerged to nibble on silver-sage tips. These lesser rabbits occupied smaller lava outcroppings that pocked the area, and now they provided food for Nick Ear and the tree bobcat.

As usual, obtaining this food became the bobcats' primary occupation, so much so that the pair was slow to notice, one afternoon, when a distant rumble signaled the approach of snowmobiles. The meanderings of a young rabbit, working its way toward their ambush site, had mesmerized them. By the time the tree bobcat came to life and made a wild sprint for the lava cave, three mechanized sleds were almost on top of her.

The snowmobilers were not out for a Sunday joyride. Each carried on the back of his machine twenty leghold traps to be set in propitious places along the stream cliffs. Bobcat season was open.

The old cat flew across the snow, exerted all of her strength, pushed herself to limits she had never before tested. But she was not built to outdistance a machine. Her lungs were too small to obtain sufficient oxygen to power her rapidly moving legs. Her narrow chest cavity pulsated with pain, and her heart, beating more rapidly than that old organ was ever meant to work, began to fibrillate.

Yet her will to live did not waver. On and on she ran, as the three machines coursed after her. Had she been cornered, she still would have found strength to make a last stand, would have fought off her pursuers with a ferocity they might not have comprehended. For they did not perceive that the same natural forces that had shaped them had made the bobcat. Their will to survive was the same as hers. And that dynamic and protean energy which had adapted and revised a tree shrew until it became a wildcat, a coyote, a bear, a man, was contained in every living being, a force too compelling to meet extinction without struggle. The bobcat would fight for more life, just as a man would.

By now the screaming machines had maneuvered into position to converge on the exhausted animal. When two managed to turn her into the path of the third, that driver jolted to a fast stop and raised his gun. But his companions shouted, fearing bullet damage to the cat's valuable pelt. In that instant, the old bobcat slipped through their dragnet.

By now she was hopelessly diverted from her course, headed away from the lava cave, running helter-skelter with no other objective than to stay ahead of her pursuers. On and on she ran, until her tongue lolled from her mouth and her sides heaved. In and out of protruding sage she wove, and still the machines kept on coming, at times careening so close behind her that snow sprayed her back. Still no fortuitous rock pile loomed before her to provide sanctuary.

In the end, the old female made it to her juniper tree. Here was safety. Eons of natural selection had endowed her with the ability to scale its twiggy obstacle course of a trunk in a matter of seconds. Like a squirrel, she spiraled up through the greenery and came to rest on a high branch, and from the security of this high perch, she looked down on her persecutors and hissed.

Below her, the men dismounted. They drew straws, and then one raised a gun and with it began to track the cat's movements as she shifted about in the treetop. His concentration was impressive. Again and again he sited her querulous face, and, again and again, before he could fire, his target would vanish into dense foliage. His companions held absolutely still. They did not want to distract him. They understood that, to the man with the gun, the hissing face on the body of the bobcat represented an important challenge. Hitting such a moving target with a bullet not only would earn him their esteem, it would also line his pockets with cash, perhaps bringing him as much as $300. To the man with the gun, the animal in the tree held no other meaning.

When he pulled the trigger, the sound of the blast traveled and reverberated and startled creatures as far away as the streambed. But the tree bobcat made no sound at all as she dropped from the juniper tree. She possessed no means of crying out. Her lower jaw had been blown away.

The men cheered and congratulated the marksman. His aim had been precise. The bobcat's pelt was undamaged. The bobcat's valuable underbelly fur was intact.

She was skinned where she fell. The man who had gunned her down worked rapidly to jerk hide from her still-warm body, pulling it off like a bloody glove being turned inside out. When this gory task was done, he washed his hands in the snow, mounted his machine, and, together with the other two trappers, roared off in the direction of the stream. From the handlebars of his sled the tree bobcat's pelt flapped and waved. And under the ancient juniper tree lay all else that remained of the old animal—a denuded carcass, a red obscenity.

Chapter 17

The men were jubilant. The tree bobcat's pelt was a windfall, one that would more than pay for the fuel they had burned reaching this remote place. Now whatever their traps would yield could be counted as straight profit.

Bobcats had become scarce. No longer were they being trapped in regions easily accessible to man. Now real effort was demanded of those determined to reap the high profits brought by their pelts. Yet there existed no shortage of people willing to make this extra effort, for no actual hardship was exacted of them. Snowmobiles put unexploited regions within reach of just about everybody, and once a string of leghold traps had been set in place, any bobcat that existed in a given area could be counted on to step into one. The animal was vulnerable in the extreme to trapping. It mattered little what kind of scent bait was used as lure, the curious bobcat felt impelled to investigate and play with the device itself. Inevitably, its probing paw would become inextricably clamped in lethal steel jaws.

The men did not stop to ponder the consequences of their actions. They were possessed by an unshakable conviction that all wildlife existed only for man to exploit. They regarded the bobcat as a renewable economic asset, just as they regarded trees or deer.

But the bobcat was not a tree, not even so renewable as a deer; the bobcat, being a predator, was not endowed with the reproductive capacity of that animal. Deer, mice, and rabbits, having been the object of predation over long ages, had evolved a high birthrate to compensate for their heavy losses. Such species produced proportionately more young the more their overall numbers were reduced. But the bobcat was not a prey species; it was a predator. Histori-

157

cally, it had never served as food for another creature and seemed not to have evolved this "compensatory birthrate." What evidence existed showed that bobcat mothers produce an average litter size of 2.8 kittens annually, regardless of how dense or sparse the animals' overall numbers. No one knew if a bobcat population could withstand the unnatural impact of being preyed upon by man.

Yet *Lynx rufus*'s apparent lack of reproductive resiliency was not only disregarded by men who trapped cats but ignored by wildlife managers across the United States. As the price paid for a prime bobcat pelt rose from $20 in 1970 to as much as $650 in 1980, the species was increasingly exploited. Bobcats grew scarce or disappeared from many parts of the animal's once widespread range.

Nick Ear, of course, experienced no endocrinological feedback on his species' lowered density. Bobcats normally avoid contact. Nick Ear's single affiliation with his kind had been with his foster mother, and even that attachment, primogenital in nature, soon would have broken off. Now, however, he missed her. When two days passed and she failed to return to the lava cave, he set off to look for her. With delicate steps, he trod across dawn-tinted drifts, following the tracks laid down by the snowmobiles. These, of course, led him to the juniper tree. A few yards short of that place, however, he stopped and hid behind a mound of snow to watch a flock of ravens erratically lifting and resetting on a blood-streaked patch of snow. He did not wish to tangle with the glossy birds over whatever

it was they had found to eat. Their movements simply held him spellbound—their flutter and flap, their strained lifts and graceful landings. Visual observations of this sort were crucial to his mental acuity. And now, after spending two days in the sensory-deprived atmosphere of a cave, he needed the restorative.

The ravens put on a good show. Even after most of their food find had been consumed, they showed no inclination to depart. One pair bounced onto the juniper tree and began courting. The female hunkered down, opened her beak, and gaped like a begging fledgling. Her mate, after a ceremonious bow, raised himself up to full stature and pretended to feed her. Some of the flock performed aerobatics, dipping and soaring and avoiding midair collision like some well-rehearsed flight corps.

Downwind, another spectator was also watching the birds. The coyote's interest in the ravens, however, was different from that of the bobcat. He felt no particular need for visual stimulation, nor did he view the birds as potential prey. To the coyote, ravens were important because they guided him to food. Cunningly, the earthbound scavenger would take a fix on a wheeling flock and so spare himself miles of random trekking across deep snow in search of winter-killed animals. The coyote and the raven had been improbable hunting partners from time immemorial.

But now the young coyote hesitated. It was not the boisterous behavior of the birds that prevented him from charging into their

159

midst to garner a share of their find. His intrusion would have created only a momentary flutter. It was the scent of gunfire, the odor of fuel, and, most of all, traces of man-smell lingering in the area that had aroused his suspicion. Though he was sorely in need of food, his fear of man was too compelling to permit him to join in the birds' feast.

Nick Ear spied the coyote and crouched. Once he had looked upon this animal as a peer, a potential playmate, had even made friendly overtures to it. But the bobcat no longer behaved so impulsively, nor was he so sociable. From hard experience, he had learned to avoid horned toads and skunks and to dispose of grasshopper mice and bats expeditiously. The tree bobcat's fear reaction had also imprinted on him the need to shun coyotes and eagles and dictated that he make a wide detour around any sign left by traveling bears or mountain lions. Nick Ear was growing into a wily bobcat, and now his discretion informed him to make a silent retreat.

He traveled low, concealing himself behind the snowy mounds created by the snowmobiles, tracks that proceeded on an undeviating course toward the streambed. From time to time, Nick Ear strayed from the packed trail to inspect some of the tree bobcat's marking stations. Her notices, however, had already grown stale.

At the rim of the canyon the tracks came to an end. Nick Ear let himself down the steep cliff face and hid in willows along the stream bank. He scanned the surrounding rocks, and, for a moment, a rustle or movement on a high ledge raised his expectations and evoked a chortle from him. But the tree bobcat did not respond to his call with the long and familiar warble that was uniquely hers. Nor did she suddenly materialize from nowhere, as was her way.

Nick Ear sat down and waited. Perhaps what he had seen on the cliff face would prove to be a meal. For several minutes, he kept an eye on the rock ledge but saw nothing out of the ordinary. Then, suddenly, he darted behind a snow-coated rock and hid. What was perched on his favorite sunning ledge was a strange bobcat, a lanky male who stood tall on long legs and stretched and yawned and looked to be making himself as much at home in the place as if he were the resident cat.

The effect this revelation had on Nick Ear's nervous system was deranging. Anxiously, he glanced about, looking for an escape route. At his precise stage of development, he could easily be intimidated. When he was younger, the unfamiliar had intrigued him, but now the appearance of anything out of the ordinary created in him a sensation of panic. At the same time, he missed the tree bobcat, craved her companionship, and a part of him longed to approach the alien cat, to touch noses with him and butt heads. All that restrained him from acting on this impulse was the recollection of the tree bobcat's own conduct toward strangers. Always, she had hidden herself and offered an intruder the opportunity to make a graceful departure. Now Nick Ear did the same.

But the lanky cat on the cliff apparently did not feel inclined to abide by any such rule of bobcat behavior. He did not depart. On the contrary, he appeared to have appropriated the place. Only a cat who had thoroughly explored his surroundings and found them to his liking could behave in so relaxed a manner, could groom himself with such an air of insouciance. The lanky stranger emanated self-confidence, and his haughty demeanor had the effect of undermining Nick Ear's own self-assurance. What's more, the stranger enjoyed a strategic advantage, for occupying an elevated position automatically conferred superior status on him. Thus, in this instance, it was the intruder and not the resident cat who enjoyed the advantage.

The lanky stranger, however, knew nothing about this. He had not caught sight of the frightened kitten who hid in the streambed. His attention was occupied with more basic matters. Mating season was at hand, and every sexually mature bobcat was beginning to make himself or herself as visible as possible. By common consent, territorial restrictions were lifted and antipathies suspended, as otherwise monastic males and normally reclusive females began wandering and trespassing and seeking contact with one another. The lanky male had come to the canyon to look for a mate.

Nick Ear watched as the male postured and paced the ledge, observed him stretch and pose and yawn and groom his elegant winter coat with lavish tongue strokes. Nick Ear gazed at the interloper until his pupils shrank to slits in their glossy yellow orbs, stared at him until the glare on the snowfield pained his eyes and forced him to seek shade. Creeping and slinking, he made his way, unobserved, to a rock overhang at the base of the cliff where he took cover out of sight of the lanky male bobcat.

But he had hardly settled himself in this hideaway when piercing screams galvanized him, readied him to take flight or fight. The cries that surrounded him offered no clue which of the two courses

would be the wiser choice, for the canyon was chiming with cat-calls. From every direction, the full-lunged clamor ululated and echoed and reverberated like some demonic chorus in a chamber of horrors.

By and by the catcalls died away, the sound decaying slowly until the high-rise rocks stood as mute as the unimaginable stretches of time that had created them. Then a rock dislodged and, during the course of its descent, struck the cliff face twice before plopping soundlessly into the snow at Nick Ear's feet. Instantly, the yowls erupted again, more ear-splitting than before—searing shrieks, an abrasive duet played by chalk and a violin's E string.

Cautiously, Nick Ear stepped from his shelter and peered upward, spied, high on the cliff face, gliding along a ledge, two stiffened ears. And heading toward these dotted pinnae, inching along the same rock catwalk, crept the lanky bobcat.

Nick Ear had never before witnessed a fight between two tomcats. For that matter, he had never even met a member of his own sex. His own body was as yet too immature to feel the rousing effects of testosterone. Two years would have to pass before that hormone would compel him to take part in the kind of battle he was about to witness.

The challengers appeared to be well matched. The lanky bobcat was the taller, an advantage emphasized by a swatch of thick hair that stood erect across his shoulders and ran the length of his spine. But his opponent, a tawny bobcat, wore the more formidable expression on his raffish face, a grimace rendered credible by a pair of frayed ears, a split lip, and a swollen eyelid. Although smaller, the tawny bobcat was obviously a force to be reckoned with.

On high, stiff legs, and at an agonizingly slow pace, the growling rivals inched toward one another. They moved along the narrow ledge a single step at a time, as haltingly as if their muscles were receiving antagonistic instructions from their brains. Their faces were contorted, their lips drawn up to reveal lethal fangs. Their ears were swiveled sideways to expose the hexing glare of bogus eyespots. Their battle song ebbed and swelled like a mighty anthem.

With precision, they enacted their pre-battle ritual. Their controlled, slow approach was necessary; it gave them the opportunity to taunt and provoke one another. Unless both cats could work up a high level of tension, neither could enter into the kind of implacable warfare that cats wage.

Mirroring and mocking, heads atilt, necks craned, the two animals gradually closed the gap that separated them. Their opening gambit had proceeded according to a fixed sequence of actions and reactions. At the same time, foresight and planning had obviously played no part in their preparations, for the contest about to be fought would take place fifty feet above the canyon floor on a ledge where there existed no room for maneuver. Had one or both cats the ability to predict the dire outcome of a battle so situated, they might have exercised restraint, at least long enough to find a more suitable arena. Perhaps they did sense the danger, but, having already worked themselves into a murderous state, they were now unable to avoid the oncoming fight.

Both froze in a crouch, each waiting for the other to make the move that would trigger attack. Meanwhile, their vocal chords were not paralyzed. Their stentorian threats grew ever more abusive, rising and falling in pitch and intensity like a widow's keen. At times, so much saliva would collect in the throat of one of the caterwaulers that he would momentarily have to fall silent to swallow, doing so with loud lip smacks. And the furious timpani of clicking teeth accompanied all the noise.

Nick Ear watched with rapidly beating heart. Locked in attack posture, the two toms looked for all the world like mounted specimens in a museum display. For nearly a full minute they held their menacing poses. Then carefully, stiffly, they raised up and stalked past one another, crossing so closely they brushed sides. Now, having exchanged positions, they turned and once again faced off.

It was the lanky cat who lunged, but the tawny cat was ready for him. In an instant he managed to flip onto his back, and with his forepaws he grappled his foe to his chest, savagely raking the attacker with his hind claws. The two rolled only once before toppling off the cliff.

Nick Ear saw them coming, saw them hurtle from above like a pair of diving falcons. He ducked under the rock overhang as the pair plummeted past and sank into snow, and he watched wide-eyed as the warring cats surfaced and bounded apart, miraculously uninjured.

For a time the canyon stood silent while the toms licked snow from their coats and recovered from the unsettling experience of falling off a cliff. Neither was so upset, however, that he was willing to call off the fight. Before long the two were parading again, swaggering and grimacing and flinging insults at one another, and all the while edging closer, closer.

This time the rivals satisfied the ritual requirements—to taunt and to posture—more quickly, and this time their place of battle presented no special hazard. The match would take place on a flat rock directly in front of Nick Ear's hiding place.

Nick Ear crept to the rear of the crevice and cowered, but there was no escape from the howls of pain that echoed throughout his hiding place as tufted ears were ripped and cheeks were slashed. Nor could he prevent the smell of spilled blood from wafting to his nostrils. The battle being waged was brutal, a test of strength and endurance that death alone seemed likely to resolve.

Each animal aimed his bite at the other's neck. Each animal parried and rolled and clasped his opponent in a battle hug. Time after time, the two cats sprang together and leaped apart. Teeth met teeth. Teeth sank into flesh. Claws slashed bellies. And throughout it all, the toms screamed and growled and snarled and hissed.

Then there was silence. Nick Ear stole to the entrance of his hiding place and peered out. The pair had broken apart, had dragged themselves in opposite directions to lick their respective wounds. But the break in hostilities was just that, merely a recess. Neither tom had conceded the battle, and before long the two combatants squared off again. The tawny cat sprang.

In this third round, the smaller cat, the tawny cat, immediately gained the advantage, and he pushed hard to finish his enemy. Repeatedly, his stabbing teeth connected with the lanky cat's head and

167

neck. With rapid paw blows the lanky cat parried and pulled back, but he was overmatched. His attacker would not let up.

The victim drew in his head and tucked it between high shoulder blades to shield his already wounded neck, but even this abject posture gained him no mercy. The two warriors were cats, not wolves or coyotes. They possessed no atavistic inclination to spare one another, no metacommunicative signal to salvage a ruptured but necessary relationship. Submissive behavior might placate a wild canid, might inhibit him from inflicting a killing bite, but it produced no such effect on a triumphing cat. Bobcat rivals were not

sometime hunting partners. Between these warring animals, no prior bond of affection existed that might now abrogate their rage. Nor did the two bear allegiance to a common pack whose unity had to be safeguarded. Each bobcat walked alone. A bobcat could afford to be ruthless.

Nevertheless, the tawny cat's savage assaults gradually subsided. He was not, however, showing mercy. Annihilation of kind was simply not in the best interest of the species, and *Lynx rufus* had evolved its own behavioral responses to protect itself from such a calamity. In order to sustain rage at a fighting threshold, a bobcat had to receive continuous threat signals from an opponent. When these ceased to be forthcoming, when a rival became too preoccupied with protecting his own neck to behave aggressively, to caterwaul and to bite, a fight would wind down.

On stiff legs the tawny cat stalked off, the victor. He did not depart the scene, however. At a short distance, he stopped and feigned interest in a bush, thus allowing the vanquished cat the opportunity to make a rapid escape.

Now the tawny male was supreme. Up the cliff face he leaped, his agility not a whit impaired by the effects of battle. As if out of insolence, he appropriated the very sunning shelf his enemy had occupied earlier in the day. His movements were stiff and exaggerated and bespoke arrogance. His wind-ruffled muttonchops were gloriously stained with blood, his frayed ears distinguished with new tatters. And his eyes shone with an affirmation of his own invincibility. He was supreme! His superiority would be passed on to any kittens born in the region come spring, for whatever females would now pass through the canyon, he would breed.

Directly below him in a rock crevice hid one frightened kitten, an end-product of some such battle fought the previous winter. The adolescent was hungry, but he dared not show himself to the formidable animal on the ledge. Throughout his young life, Nick Ear had relied on the tree bobcat to guide him through all threatening crises. Now he listened for her chortle, looked for her to put in her silent appearance. But the kitten waited in vain. The tree bobcat, together with all of her wild wisdom, had perished from the earth. All that remained of her was a scrap of belly fur destined to become a coat sleeve.

Nick Ear had no way of knowing it, but he was now a bobcat on his own.

Chapter 18

A shooting star beamed its ancient news across light-years of vanished time, but the stream bobcat did not glance up as she wended her way through a glade of willow stems that bordered the waterway. She was heading toward a cross point, an ice bridge strong enough to bear her light step. In the night air, static electricity crackled and raised her fur, but her spirit remained unruffled. On through the darkness she glided, sidestepping obstacles, guided through close places by face whiskers that could detect even slight changes in air currents. Nothing distracted her. When one of her oversized paws punched through crusted snow, her march proceeded without interruption. The female was resolute. A male had screamed, beckoned her, filled her with intention. Nothing—no geologic barrier, no natural calamity, no physical discomfort—could deter her from journeying toward that concupiscent call.

Only to leave her mark in the snow did she occasionally pause, genuflecting cursorily as she deposited each yellow stain. In the morning, these notices of her passage, posted at twenty-foot intervals, might be discovered by some visiting tom equally in need of genetic continuity. Both sexes would be traveling now, and the female could not risk being missed on home ground while off searching for sexual encounter elsewhere. The stream bobcat was in estrus.

From the opposite bank, Nick Ear watched, eyes shining with gathered light, tracking the shadowy silhouette as it slipped in and out of silver reeds. The kitten's body was tense with anticipation. For nearly a week now, he had remained in the canyon, waiting for the tree bobcat to reappear. Each night when darkness provided him with cover, he crept from his rock shelter at the base of the cliff

and slipped into a clump of frosted vegetation along the stream bank. There, concealed from the terrible eyes of the tawny male, he fed on luckless mice and scanned the cliff face for some sign of his missing companion. But every movement that caught his attention inevitably proved to be the pacing of the restless tom, who kept to the high ledges and, intermittently, startled all the canyon creatures with his terrible screams.

Now, once again from a high dark place, the male began to rhapsodize, shrieking his invitation to any and all females within earshot to come and relieve his priapism. His cries set rimrocks ringing in sympathetic vibration, like rubbed crystal, and the cacophony jarred a great stalactite of an icicle loose from a rock face, sent it spiraling downward to spear a bush below.

The stream bobcat heard these sounds and quickened her pace. Even in her haste, however, she did nothing that might compromise her safety. Secretiveness was integral to her nature, and whatever vegetative cover was proximate, she used, detouring through it. Where no such natural blinds existed, she crossed open places as swiftly and evanescently as a shadow floats past the moon's face.

Nick Ear crouched. When the stream bobcat dropped from the opposite bank onto the stream ice, excitement generated in his breast, rose like a gasp, and escaped from his throat as a small sound. Surely this feline figure heading toward the thicket in which he lay hidden was the tree bobcat. Soon the two would be reunited, would butt heads, rub cheeks, touch noses.

During their separation, he had missed these affectionate exchanges. Although he had nearly attained adult stature and by now would have almost equaled his late foster mother in size, he had not outgrown his need for her. Yet, as the approaching figure grew more distinguishable, Nick Ear's high anticipation changed to queasy dread. The kitten's bobbed tail twitched convulsively. The animal about to discover him was not the tree bobcat!

A band of fur running the length of his spine rose high, allowing frigid air to riffle down to his hide. Fine muscles in his four big paws tightened, unsheathing eighteen razor-sharp claws. Adrenaline flooded his body, readying him for action. Encounter with the stranger was already inescapable.

The meeting took place suddenly. In a single leap the stream bobcat put herself up on the bank, as lightly as snow is lifted in an updraft. And she and Nick Ear were face to face.

The abruptness of their encounter insulted both animals. It is not in the nature of the bobcat to surprise its own kind. Normally, strangers keep a respectful distance, slowly assessing one another while deciding on which course of action to take—whether to pass with caution, make a discreet withdrawal, or obey that most reliable of impulses and remain hidden. But now, caught inside a critical distance, neither Nick Ear nor the stream bobcat could consider any one of these options. Even quick retreat was foreclosed to them. At such proximity, abrupt flight on the part of one cat might trigger a chase response in the other. For a long moment, the two stood and stared. They were at an impasse, and they quivered with tension.

Nick Ear was the first to react. He spat—screwed up his face, laid back his ears, and hissed. The stream bobcat was not so impetuous. She waited for an opening, studied her opponent, paused to calculate her best move. But the kitten possessed no such poise. With paws spread wide, he reared on his hind legs and swatted the air. His wild punches were feints and failed to connect with anything, but this he did not seem to notice. As he danced about, he seemed to be playing for time, trying to create space for himself to make an adroit retreat. His flailing behavior, however, only served to expose his ineptitude, to inform the stream bobcat that she was the superior animal, that she could dispose of Nick Ear in one swift attack. At any instant, she could seize him by the neck and cripple or kill him.

Yet, paradoxically, even while the kitten's poor fighting form made of him a vulnerable target, it also granted him a kind of protection. A more skilled fighter might have provoked the adult female to greater fury. But Nick Ear's moves were not offensive ones, only defensive paw blows, and these did not arouse the stream bobcat to do her worst. As a result, she responded in kind, striking only with her paws and not with her jaws.

With a low swipe at Nick Ear's staggering hind feet, she deftly unbalanced him. The surprised kitten leaped backward, spinning broadside as he traveled through the air. His face contorted, his eyes glazed, his ears flattened until they disappeared in raised fur. But the adult female was not intimidated by grimaces. With very little effort she had established her supremacy, and now she looked upon the kitten as a mere annoyance, an obstacle that impeded her progress through the canyon. She would promptly dispense with him.

Under ordinary conditions, an invading cat would suffer such anxiety in an unfamiliar setting that it could easily be intimidated and run off by a resident cat. By the same token, the resident cat, feeling fully confident in its habitual surroundings, almost without exception would prevail over an invader. But in this particular showdown, the resident bobcat was an adolescent, entirely lacking in tactical skill. Nick Ear had never before fought another cat. And this disadvantage was further compounded by the stream bobcat's elevated self-esteem, a condition perhaps induced by the unusual level of hormones that now flooded her system. Moreover, she was determined to remain in this area from which a mating call had been sounded. Given these conditions, no cat could make her back down.

So when Nick Ear once again reared and slashed at air, the stream bobcat decided to put an end to the charade. An ominous sound gurgled in her throat as she slowly rotated her ears until the ersatz gaze of two white spots stared at her young opponent. Then, swinging her head from side to side, she invited Nick Ear to do real battle, to fight her with fang as well as claw. Nick Ear panicked, drew himself into a ball, rolled onto his back, and kicked wildly in the air with four paws spread wide as hands. Thus he demonstrated, once again, his inability to counter an offensive with an offensive.

Had the stream bobcat been intent on combat, the young male would not have escaped without injury. But more pressing matters demanded her attention. Abruptly, her temper subsided, and, artfully, she dismissed the irksome kitten, releasing him from her charmed presence. She did this by moving to one side and focusing all of her attention on a particular spot of ground. While she sniffed and examined this quite ordinary place, the kitten put distance between them.

The stream bobcat's technique for ending the conflict was not improvised by herself. It had been perfected over eons of time by uncountable generations of battling felines. Now it was coded into the genes of the cat family and insured the animals at least one bloodless technique for winding down disputes. Endowed as the bobcat was with the ability to kill, the species needed some such behavioral mechanism to safeguard its continued survival.

Nick Ear did not run far. He was frightened and flustered, yet he was already too much of a bobcat to yield his Eden to another cat after a single defeat. Although he might soon adopt the nomadic life-style assigned by nature to yearling members of his species, ma-

turation rather than force would likely instigate the behavior. For the present, he took shelter in a rock crevice and stared off into space, like some badly directed actor trying to put on a show of indifference. Growing up was indeed a complicated process.

Meanwhile, the stream bobcat wasted no time moving to the exact spot Nick Ear had vacated, and she touched her nose to it. The pheromones he had released there, however, failed to arouse her interest. The exudate whispered only of her opponent's fear and lacked the musky redolence her nose would have relished.

Slowly, she lifted her head and cast an impassive glance in the direction taken by the vanquished kitten. Then, with arrogant bearing, she stepped across his imprint in the snow and deposited two drops of urine over it. This done, she moved off, winding through slender willow stems as regally as a tiger glides through a bamboo copse.

The incident was closed. In her present state of sexual readiness, the stream bobcat could waste no more time making either war or peace with an immature male. Once again her single-minded aim asserted full claim to her attention. She would rendezvous with that full-voiced tom whose song had lured her to cross the stream. Nick Ear was forgotten. He held no further interest for her, aroused no associations in her. Months ago, the taste of his birth fluid had faded from her memory. The stream bobcat had failed to recognize her own.

Chapter 19

In previous years the stream bobcat had not needed to stray off home ground to find a mate. The mountain male had always put in his appearance days before the stream bobcat was ready to let him do more than circle and sniff her. For his punctuality, the tom was rewarded with much abuse, for until her estrus peaked and she was ready to copulate, the stream bobcat behaved as capriciously as Circe, crying seductively and pushing her head and body along the ground in direct view of the tantalized male. But woe to him should he interpret her sensual writhing as a bid for his immediate services; any premature advances on his part would be met with furious and rapid paw blows.

Nevertheless, each year without fail the mountain bobcat had arrived ahead of time—at least a week before the stream bobcat would submit to being mounted. It was a matter of expediency that he be present during this early phase of her breeding cycle. For a moment would arrive, and quite abruptly, when her provocative behavior would change to earnest demand. And when this happened, he could not keep her waiting. He had not fathered every one of her three litters by being late.

This year, however, the mountain tom had not put in an appearance at all, and as time passed and the stream bobcat's restlessness increased, she had set off in search of her tardy mate. For several days and as many nights, she had paced and called along the lower slopes of his lofty home. But the mountain male, now nine months dead, could not be summoned by plaintive yowls. At last she abandoned the effort and hurried off in another direction. Mating season was of short duration. No more time could be spent in pursuit of an unresponsive male, however preferred he might be to other toms.

Had she been a logical, reasoning animal, she would have headed directly for the canyon, deducing that the year-round water there would likely attract thirsty visitors. Eventually, she did set off in that direction, motivated by simple memory. The dim recollection of fecal deposits, unburied and foreign, all at once compelled her to thread her way to the stream. En route, her tufted ears perked up and began to swivel. She had heard the mating call of the tawny male.

The stream bobcat did not know the tom who at that moment was producing the banshee wails. He had come to the streambed from a faraway place, had traveled more than fifty miles in search of a female. Everywhere in the state, bobcat numbers had dwindled and sexually mature animals were on the move, crossing unfamiliar terrain, encountering unfamiliar animals.

The sharp decline of *Lynx rufus* was not unprecedented, nor was it an entirely unnatural event. In the wake of rabbit fluctuations, bobcats peaked and crashed cyclically. Within limits, these occasional population depressions were even beneficial to the species. For when sparsely distributed, bobcats were compelled to seek mates far from home and so would introduce new genes into isolated populations in need of outbreeding.

But this year, coincident with a natural die-off, fur trappers were also taking a high toll of the animal. Moreover, the traplines they planted across the country hindered survivors from mating and fostering the species' comeback, for it was the sexually active cats who inadvertently became the trappers' primary victims. Not many mate seekers were making it safely across the vast stretches mined with leghold sets. One tom who had made it, however, was the tawny male, and now his dauntless energy and good luck were about to be rewarded. He had spied the stream bobcat gliding along the canyon floor and, with a spider's indifference to gravity, had bounded down the cliff face as if secured by that creature's towline.

Dawn had obliterated all but a scattering of stars from the sky when the two cats, gray forms, eased together. Whatever reticence the tawny tom normally experienced in making the acquaintance of another cat no longer obtained. Assertively, he approached the female, driven by the unconscious imperative to introduce his partic-

ular genes into this desert population, which, over the past several years, had been the exclusive breeding domain of the mountain male. The two cats touched noses, rubbed cheeks, then circled, each intent on inspecting the other's anal region while attempting not to submit to the same indignity.

The stream bobcat was at the peak of estrus and could have mated at once. Even so, she would not dispense with the rituals cats normally perform prior to copulation. With sinuous movements, she rolled on the snow, first rubbing her face against the cold stuff, then pushing her shoulders and flanks across a drift in clear view of the wide-eyed male. Yet when he presumed to accommodate her, when he gripped her neck skin in his teeth and tried to mount her, she slashed him with her claws, then turned and fled.

The tom was undaunted by the rebuff and pursued her. As he loped along, a murmuring serenade poured from his throat, a low-keyed, insistent kind of song that had a calming effect on the jumpy female. In a few minutes she stopped running and looked back. Then, slowly, she lowered the front part of her body in a camel bow, while her quivering hindquarters remained upright and her raised tail flopped from one side to the other.

This posture was interpreted by the male as an invitation for him to mount, and he rushed to do so. Once again he seized her neck scruff in his teeth and tried to straddle her. But the stream bobcat would have none of him. She whirled and slashed at him with ten fully extended front claws. Then she ran fifty yards downstream without slackening her pace. When at last she did come to a halt, it was to ascertain that the tawny male was still in pursuit. And for several seconds, while he decreased the distance that separated them, she nonchalantly washed herself.

By now the male was becoming more artful in his approach. This time he made no abrupt move that might again trigger the high-strung female to take flight. This time he maintained a respectful distance and seated himself, as if he had suddenly fathomed the role that nature had assigned to his sex. During this phase of courtship, while the female writhed and cried and worked herself into a state of sexual receptivity, all that was required of him was his stimulating presence. Not until she was fully aroused would his direct advances be tolerated.

So the male waited. From time to time, however, he could not refrain from taking the measure of the female's excitement. Tenta-

tively, he would approach and sniff the ruff of fur on her neck, withdrawing swiftly when her paw blows informed him of his miscalculation. Once, the stream bobcat did hold still long enough for him to grasp her neck skin firmly in his teeth and fling one forepaw across her body, but then she reacted as before with loud snarls and a display of unsheathed claws. Yet her resistance was gradually eroding. For, soon thereafter, the tawny tom was permitted to climb on her back and knead her hips with his hind feet until her lumbar region was almost elevated to the angle necessary for mating to take place. Then, at the critical moment, the stream bobcat refused to lift her tail, and, abruptly, she twisted onto her back so that the male could not maintain his grip on her neck. For this, his boldest move yet, he was not punished. The stream bobcat was apparently becoming compliant.

Nevertheless, she was not yet ready to mate. First she led the persevering tom a mile up the canyon on a flirt-chase that unfolded according to behavioral patterns coded into the cats' psyches. Whenever the male failed to keep pace with the fleeing female, she slowed down and looked back at him until he caught up. Whenever she grew fearful that her suitor might be losing interest in this game of pursuit, she stopped altogether, cast him a coy glance, and cried out. The male, of course, needed no such encouragement.

Finally, even the stream bobcat grew weary of running and stopped, and the male, after seating himself a few yards off, resumed his crooning. Rhythmically, as if to his tune, the stream bobcat brushed her body back and forth against a boulder. Then she dropped onto the snow and once again slid about and cried.

This time, however, whenever the stream bobcat closed her eyes in euphoric self-sensing, the tawny tom seized the opportunity to steal a few feet nearer. And before her eyes had again opened, he took care to be found seated and staring off into space. Thus, he closed the gap that separated him from the capricious female who was ready to mate, but not quite willing to do so.

All the while he continued to serenade her in a modulated voice that contained the merest suggestion of a purr. And this mating song further aroused the stream bobcat, until at last she was ready to let herself be seized by the nape, was able to let herself be clasped around the middle. Crouching on her front legs, she elevated her hindquarters, and, while her back paws trod the ground, the male inserted his penis.

Coitus lasted only ten seconds. After enduring only a few pelvic thrusts, the female began to shriek. Horny spines on the tom's sex organ, perhaps holdfasts necessary to secure the pair during ejaculation, hurt her, and she reacted violently to the pain, springing at the male and attacking him with tooth as well as claw. But the tawny bobcat had anticipated her reaction and jumped clear of the bundle of fury that hurtled toward him. He was not an inexperienced breeder.

The stream bobcat licked her swollen vulva and rested on her side. The male bided his time, lingered by a boulder, and waited for the stream bobcat to renew her invitation to him to mate. He had been through all of this before and seemed to know that soon again his services would be in demand. When the female next would indicate her willingness to mate, they would do so promptly, with little preliminary activity.

And indeed, coitus did take place again soon, preceded only by perfunctory resistance on the part of the female. Although this second mating was as brief and apparently uncomfortable for the stream bobcat as their initial union had been, and although it, too, concluded with a ferocious attack on the tawny tom, afterward both cats seemed equally eager to enter into repeated coitus. And so, over the course of the day and throughout the night, as quickly as the pair recovered from one violent copulation experience, they entered into the process all over again.

In the end, it was the male who tired of mating and took his leave, and it was the female who pursued him. Flirting and crying, crouching and waving her stubby tail, the stream bobcat ran after the tawny tom and teased him to mount her. Reluctantly, he did so for one last time. Then he departed at a dead run.

Their final union had been a gratuitous act. The stream bobcat was already impregnated. Embryonic cells, rapidly dividing within her body, would soon order themselves into complex arrangements that, within a few weeks' time, would serve as organs and muscles and skin and bone for three baby bobcats. Nature had had her way. The species would persist.

Chapter 20

Manacled on a narrow ledge, a rough-legged hawk struggled to free itself; it fluttered and postured and clicked its beak at the three men who approached. And each time the enraged bird drew itself up to flap its mighty wings, the leghold trap that fettered it bit more deeply into its foot.

The men stopped and watched, but they made no move to open the device and release the hawk. The bird would never again be able to hunt; its talons were mangled beyond nature's power to heal, and so the animal would have to be destroyed. The men delayed. The opportunity to observe such a magnificent bird at close range was not likely to occur soon again. When it flapped its wings, they fanned to a four-foot spread. But, finally, the men acted. Armed with heavy rocks, they moved swiftly and, working in unison, bludgeoned the raptor. The bird did not die quickly.

The trappers were one week late making their rounds, and their tardiness was illegal. A state regulation required that every trap be visited within seventy-two hours of being set just so such unintended victims as the rough-legged hawk might be released. But the men had ignored this regulation, and, in so doing, they had run slight risk of being apprehended. The Idaho Department of Fish and Game was not staffed to keep the state's vast wilderness under constant surveillance, and the likelihood of anybody's traps being discovered, let alone monitored over a three-day period by one of the overworked game wardens, was as remote as were the places in which most traps were concealed. In short, the trap regulation was unenforceable.

Without show of emotion, the men disposed of the hawk, pitched its remains over the cliff and moved on. The bird could not have been spared, regardless of how soon they had returned to inspect their traps. It had been too seriously injured. And so, despite the fact that the men admired the species, they felt no guilt over the necessity of having to kill it.

Now they got on with the business of locating and resetting their many traps. Three more were found to contain unwanted animals—a horned lark, a jackrabbit, and a pack rat. But unlike the hawk, these commonplace species failed to arouse the men's interest. All were dead and had been so for several days. Birds had fed on the jackrabbit carcass, and, as a result, its pelt, ordinarily of some value, was ruined. The men tossed it onto the bank, together with the bodies of the other so-called trash animals.

If the trappers felt any remorse over the wasted life, they did not show it. They cursed the "worthless" creatures who, by springing their baited sets, had precluded valuable fur-bearing animals from stepping into them. Even less sympathetic were the expressions they directed toward the game department officials who had promulgated the seventy-two-hour visitation rule. They viewed themselves as freedom-loving Americans, unsentimental and knowledgeable, and they resented government interference of any kind. They dismissed this particular regulation as the work of environmentalists, "bleeding hearts from the city who never laid eyes on a coyote or a bobcat." And so they inspected their traps when it suited them to do so, and by their defiance proved to their own satisfaction that they were their own men.

In actual fact, it probably mattered little that these individuals had chosen to flout the law. Seventy-two hours was no tolerable stretch of time for an animal to endure entrapment. Many states required that sets be visited every twenty-four hours; if released within a day of capture, an animal stood some chance of surviving the ordeal of being held fast by unyielding steel jaws. But with the passage of three days and three nights, clamped paws grew gangrenous from lack of blood, animals froze, died of shock, or succumbed to dehydration. Some were even discovered and eaten by predators. Worst of all was the fate of those coyotes and foxes who became so frenzied by restraint that they gnawed off their own paws to gain freedom. After a lapse of three days and three nights, a trapper might return to find only a leg or a paw in his trap.

From a secret vantage point, Nick Ear observed the men, watched them bait their deadly devices with cotton wads soaked in strong scent, looked on as they positioned their traps where signs indicated the presence of bobcats. Had Nick Ear been a coyote, he would afterward have avoided these places; he would have been wary of every strange object he encountered, been ruled by a suspicious rather than a curious nature. But he was a cat, and so his investigative urge was stronger than his canniness. Though, like every bobcat, he avoided contact with human beings and was unsurpassed in his ability to conceal himself, he failed to extend this mistrust of man to the objects man left behind him. And so Nick Ear, like all of his kind, was a likely candidate for the fur market.

But for the moment he was safe. He had put himself beyond notice of the trappers by crossing to the stream bobcat's side of the canyon at the first sound of their approach, had concealed himself in a cave on the facing cliff. The men, fearing that a thaw might melt the thin stream ice before their next visit, had made the decision not to plant traps along this far bank. Nick Ear would not be discovered.

The morning was beautiful, blue and crisp, a fine day to spend out-of-doors. The men laughed and joked as they baited their traps, and their banter allowed the young bobcat to monitor their shifting whereabouts. Like the noisy chatter of birds, their talkativeness was alien to his own silent nature. When he felt exuberant, he ran up a cliff. Cold air and the stimulation of natural surroundings apparently inspired a vocal response in man, and on this day the three trappers, delighting in the beauty of their surroundings, attributed their high spirits to the particular "sport" in which they were engaged. To them, killing animals was synonymous with the wholesome outdoor life.

But their presence in the canyon had no similarly uplifting effect on the creatures who dwelt there. None stirred while *Homo sapiens*, most feared of predators, was in their midst. Only a single bird briefly revealed its presence by sounding an alarm cry before flying off to safer realms. And until the men climbed out, taking an easy ascent route to the cliff top where they had parked their snowmobiles, Nick Ear crouched and remained motionless.

It was not an easy feat for a bobcat to remain still in a cave he had not previously explored. Being in unfamiliar surroundings was unnerving. But Nick Ear's fear of man was great and eclipsed his deep need to know his immediate environs. Until the sound of their

departing machines puttered into silence, he kept them under surveillance and suppressed his impulse to look about the cave.

The men were disappointed. No furbearer had stepped into any of their leghold devices. Now, as they rebaited and reset traps, placing them in more strategic locations, they made bets on which traps would hold bobcats on their return. When that might be was open to speculation. None of the men was a professional trapper; none would allow this avocation to take precedence over his job or private life. Moreover, their reluctance to make frequent trap checks was now reinforced by their lack of success. It did not occur to them that the empty leghold devices might signal a serious decline in the population of the fur-bearing animals they sought to catch.

When the men had gone, Nick Ear at last felt free to explore the cave in which he had taken refuge. The first thing he examined was the heap of bone fragments, rodent teeth, and bird claws that lay in one corner. This midden of refuse told him the cave had served other bobcats before him, and the information was not reassuring. Next he discovered a potential food source. In a crack in the cave wall there lay coiled a number of hibernating snakes. The reptiles made no response when Nick Ear deftly fished one out and ate it.

Afterward he felt better. His diet during the past two days had consisted of only four voles, and now the sensation of a full stomach was almost uncomfortable. The young bobcat was growing larger and needed increasing amounts of food to sustain him, but only once since the disappearance of the tree bobcat had he happened upon what might have been a substantial meal, had it not turned out to be inedible.

At first the trapped rabbit had seemed hardly different from the food donations his foster mother had from time to time deposited at his feet. But there *was* a difference: This rabbit had been dead too long a time and was frozen as hard as the bleached driftwood upon which he honed his claws. Although on some earlier day, magpies had managed to peck holes in its hide, Nick Ear could not bite off a single piece. With his best shearing teeth, his carnassials, he worried the carcass and chomped on it from the side of his short mouth. But he was unable to tear away an ingestible bite.

A coyote could have done it. A coyote possessed the right equipment to attack frozen meat—a long jaw and formidable molars behind his carnassials. With these grinders, a coyote could gnaw on an intact carcass until it yielded a manageable chunk. A coyote was designed to scavenge on winter-killed animals, for that was his proper food niche. A bobcat, on the other hand, had to go right on hunting in subfreezing weather.

When Nick Ear finished eating the snake, he returned to the cave opening and glanced about. The view aroused no recollection of his past, failed to evoke memories of a time when this same rock recess had served as his first home. For during that infantile stage of his life, he had taken no note of such things as distant landmarks or outlooks. Now, however, reference points had become significant to the young cat and he registered the view. When his reconnoitering was done, he stretched and lay down and soon would have drifted off to sleep had he not caught sight of movement on the opposite bank. Motion always brought him to full alert, and now he stared with unblinking intensity, stared and waited with exquisite patience, until he was able to decipher the cause of the commotion.

Nick Ear had not been the only bobcat who, on that winter day, had watched the men set their traps. At the first sound of their approach, the tawny tom had also taken refuge in rocks. But he had been caught with short warning and, as a consequence, had been forced to squeeze his body into a nearby cliff crack, there to remain in close proximity to the men throughout the morning.

The situation had greatly stressed the bobcat's nervous system, and this tension had been intensified when a dead hawk landed directly in his narrow line of vision. The tantalized tom could scarcely contain his impulse to abandon his hiding place and leap upon the bird. But his fear of man was craven, and so he remained in his cramped quarters, his pulse racing, his tail twitching, saliva pouring from his limp mouth. For some time after the trappers had left, he did not emerge from his rock cover. At last, though, he crept out and looked around. The dead hawk still obsessed him. When he had satisfied himself that nothing in his immediate surroundings had been altered, he moved to the big bird and began to strip it of feathers.

The tawny tom was ravenous. Two days of mating, followed by such a stressful morning, had left him enervated. Now he gorged, sometimes gagging on the oversized bites he tore off and swallowed. Not until every edible part of the carcass had been consumed did he pause to scrub away the blood that smeared his scarred face. Afterward, he retired to a rock slab to sun and sleep for the rest of the day, while hawk matter gradually became transformed into bobcat flesh.

When the sun set, the tom awakened and, feeling ready to mate again, declared this desire with his usual stridency. But when only the echo of his shrill call answered him, he climbed to the top of the cliff and trotted across the desert, heading for new mating ground.

Nick Ear watched him depart. Not until the following day, however, did he return to the far side of the canyon. Meanwhile, he kept an eye on the place, watching for the possible return of the big cat. At last, assured that the far bank was once again unoccupied, he crossed the stream.

No matter how alarming had been the events of the past few days, the young bobcat preferred to inhabit familiar ground. Moreover, his curiosity, titillated by what he had witnessed, now demanded satisfaction. His first act was to sniff the many tracks left by the tawny tom. Then he inspected the frozen carcasses of the rabbit, the pack rat, and the horned lark, in that order. Once again, he tried to obtain a meal from the jackrabbit's hard remains, but once again the effort proved futile. Next he clamored up the cliffside and investigated the crevice in which the tawny tom had hidden himself. The scent of the big cat's fear still lingered in the tight space. After having thoroughly checked out his surroundings, Nick Ear leaped onto an overhang that jutted out into space.

Less and less now did he give thought to the tree bobcat; more and more he was content to be in his own company. A sudden burst of high spirits set him to leaping. Throughout most of the night, he pranced and chortled, as if in celebration of his own homecoming. And in the morning he slept, slept the sound sleep of a protected house cat. The tawny tom was gone; the men, too, had departed; his stomach was full; all was well in his world.

But the kitten's life was in peril. It was only a matter of time before he would come upon a strong-smelling cotton wad, and the unfamiliar object would demand to be investigated, manipulated, batted with a wide paw. His bobcat world was beset with dangers for which evolution had not prepared him. Neither peerless agility nor formidable claws could protect a mortal cat from the lethal metal devices that lay concealed about him.

When the sun rose, Nick Ear recalled his snake meal of two days earlier and, like a farm cat who knows where the cows are milked, set his course for the cave. But, as he let himself down the cliff face, suddenly he was stopped short. His fur raised high like the quills of a startled porcupine, and a sound escaped him as sibilant as the hiss of an angry bull snake. He and the stream bobcat had once again come face to face, and this time their unexpected encounter had occurred on a ledge twenty feet above the canyon floor.

The stream bobcat made no response to Nick Ear's vocal challenge, did not even rise up on her feet. Nick Ear edged backward. Still the stream bobcat remained motionless, and instead of growling at the brazen kitten who had almost dropped onto her back, she uttered a plaintive mew. But even this uncharacteristic and nonthreatening sound caused Nick Ear to recoil; he jumped to a higher ledge and peered down on the cat who was his natural mother. Her behavior was not at all in accord with his feline expectations. She seemed totally indifferent to his presence as she lay huddled and unmoving in a too narrow place. For what had befallen the stream bobcat was so devastating that even a confrontation with another cat now failed to arouse any response in her. All night she had struggled to free her toes from a trap that had slammed on them with the merciless force of a car door. No fight was left in her. No longer did she try to shift her weight in an effort to obtain relief from the hard steel on which she was forcibly bedded. With her free paw she had tried to claw open the device that was restraining her, had broken a tooth biting at it, but the insentient trap would not yield up her paw. And because every movement she made worsened her pain, at last she had resigned herself to her agony and had grown inert, awaiting a fate that was slow in coming.

And now for a second night she lay in the trap and suffered; now for a second night she remained in her cramped posture while stars rotated across the sky. Her pain seemed to calm; her paw, lacking blood, had grown numb and was dying. Then, as light began to streak the eastern sky, announcing the dawn of her last day on earth, the stream bobcat became agonizingly aware of her vulnerability. Where she lay, she was open to view, could not escape, could not defend herself, and, most unbearable to her bobcat way of thinking, she could not hide. Her response to this torment was to sink into shock, and while her blood pressure dropped and her body grew limp, Nick Ear remained on the ledge above and watched.

Nothing in the young bobcat's experience, nothing in his heredity, instructed him how to respond to the sight of another bobcat in

distress. Yet, inexplicably, he remained near the trapped animal. He made no solicitous gesture. He was not endowed with a mother cat's care-giving instincts, nor did he feel any impulse to offer solace by rubbing against the wretched animal. She was a stranger. Still, he lingered, pacing and chirping and behaving in an agitated manner Perhaps in his compulsive fixation on the stream bobcat's plight there existed the potential for an altruistic response, for bobcats have been known to bring food to trapped bobcats, and scientists no longer view such impulses as exclusively human.

At sundown the stream bobcat died. Her recent mating activity had drained her adrenaline reserves; she could not survive a siege of shock. And with her passing, three embryo kittens were also denied the promise of life. After the stream bobcat had been dead for an hour, Nick Ear dropped down to inspect her remains. In short order, he determined that she no longer bore watching. He lived in the present, and now stomach contractions signaled him to get on with the unending business of food finding.

Off he set for the cave, stopping only once to investigate the scent signature of the deceased stream bobcat where she had recently deposited it on a bush. The potion was strong, yet it stirred no passion in the immature animal. Nor did it serve to repel him. The stream bobcat was no more, and Nick Ear, dimly aware of this, invaded her home range with confidence. In a series of bold leaps, he put himself up on the cave ledge. Then he turned to survey the canyon.

The young bobcat did not make a deliberate, conscious decision to remain on the far bank. He was, after all, a cat. But his mental processes served his survival. What bound him to the place was his own opportunistic nature, his response to the knowledge that there was a plentiful supply of hibernating snakes there. That such a move happened to put him out of the way of leghold traps was only a fortuitous circumstance. He was not a calculating animal, not a clever coyote, who, after observing one of his kind in a trap, ever afterward would avoid falling victim to the same fate. Nick Ear was as naive and unsuspecting as if he had never borne witness to the stream bobcat's suffering and death.

So it was chance, blind chance, that now spared him. But on some later day, chance would as likely finger him for destruction. For next year and the year after that, trappers would return to the canyon. Next year and the year after that, pelt prices would soar ever higher, luring ever more people to seek profit from the fur of the bobcat. The likelihood that an individual animal could escape indefinitely such commercial pressure was as dim as man's awareness of the consequences of his actions.

But for now, Nick Ear snared and ate a snake. Then he made himself comfortable. What lay ahead could not affect his present, and he was incapable of speculating on the future. He did not even know he had fallen heir to an entire canyon. For come spring, the rock recesses that pocked the cliff walls would shelter no newborn kittens; come summer, the stream would reflect no pansy faces of curious young; and come fall, the wet banks would record no clawless prints of awkward mousers. All the breeding females were dead. Nick Ear was the lone occupant of a vast territory.

Author's Note

Following the shadowy trail of "the cat that walks by its lone" was a lot harder than I had anticipated. My past experience tracking wild horses, coyotes and key deer had not prepared me for the hurdles I would have to surmount to find and observe bobcats in the wild. Though every species possesses clever strategies by which to maintain privacy, the bobcat excels at the art of being a recluse. For months I pursued sign of this animal before catching my first glimpse of one. Assiduously, I followed tracks, discovered still-warm kills, hid by scratching posts, sniffed marking stations, sifted fecal material and planted road-killed rabbits in propitious places. Resolutely, I peered into bat caves, sidestepped rattlesnakes and scaled cliff faces. The bobcat's choice of habitat, I soon discovered, presented a number of hazards to a clumsy biped. More than once I found myself awkwardly balanced on a cliff ledge within striking range of a rattlesnake.

Of course none of that time was lost. An animal's story is legibly written on the path it walks—if one takes notice. Meanwhile I read everything I could find on bobcats and on wild felines in general. And I visited and observed every captive bobcat I could track down. I even managed to meet Dr. Paul Leyhausen, the German ethologist whose knowledge and studies of cat behavior helped me to interpret what eventually I was able to see. And I repeatedly returned to wilderness areas to search for the elusive bobcat.

Then, unexpectedly, I began to meet with occasional successes. In four states—Idaho, Arizona, California and Florida—I encountered bobcats that allowed themselves to be viewed. Ironically,

195

whenever a bobcat did begin to tolerate my presence, it hardly seemed perturbed by my proximity. This suggested to me that *I* must have been the object of *its* study long before the roles were reversed.

In the end, after nearly three years of effort, I found I had amassed a great deal of information. But I was then presented with a dilemma: My observations had come from diverse localities and I was at a loss how to organize them into a cohesive and meaningful account of bobcat life. Each incident seemed to require a lengthy explanation of the setting and circumstances that surrounded it. At the same time I could also see how these isolated pieces of behavior added up to a pattern of living that guaranteed the species' survival. The problem was: How to communicate this insight in a simple manner?

The solution I hit upon was to create a composite picture of all I had seen, and set it in a single place. By moving all my bobcat observations to Idaho, I was able to make a meaningful whole out of many hard-earned pieces. I could show how the bobcat's lifestyle functions to promote the species survival within a discrete population.

To construct a realistic demography for my cast of cat characters, I relied on data already collected. Because I set my story in Dr. Theodore Bailey's research area in Idaho, I used his findings to describe home range sizes, land tenure, prey preference and kitten survival. It was helpful too that I had spent a long hot summer observing bobcats in that same place. By the same token, I disregarded telemetry studies conducted in other climes where bobcat's land requirements have been demonstrated to be greater or lesser or where prey availability differs.

It is my profound hope that this approach does not disturb readers, but instead promotes clarity and a better understanding of the connectedness of all species. I hope, too, that Nick Ear's story will help to increase public sensitivity toward all wild beings, whose impulse to stay alive is as powerful as our own.

HOPE RYDEN
April, 1990

A Bobcat Update-1990

In 1981 when this book was first published, a vogue for long-haired "fun furs" was taking a high toll of North America's bobcats. At the time, a single pelt, which prior to 1970 had sold at fur auctions for under $20, could bring as much as $650. How the bobcat had acquired such monetary value confounded professional trappers, for its fur is inferior—weak and brittle and sheds easily. Moreover, it does not take dye well. Prior to the mid-seventies, bobcat fur had been used almost exclusively for trim.

Ironically, it was the passage of the Endangered Species Act in 1973, together with the conclusion of an international agreement to regulate trade in endangered species—the CITES Treaty—that inadvertently created a demand for bobcat fur. In addition to the United States, 66 nations had signed the CITES Treaty, which, among other things, banned export of vanishing cheetah, leopard and ocelot. Furriers, unhappy over the loss of those spotted furs, wasted no time finding a substitute—the North American bobcat. Eleven matched belly skins pieced together into a full-length coat and bearing the euphemistic label, "lynx cat" or "cat lynx," began to appear in fashion salons throughout Europe and in Japan. In no time bobcat coats were so popular abroad that 80 to 90 percent of the annual take was exported. To a lesser degree "lynx-cat" coats were also sold in the United States. But here people were not so quick to pay the exorbitant prices being asked for such an inferior fur—$8,000 and up!

Trappers, of course, were delighted by the unexpected bonanza and they began baiting their sets to catch bobcats. They were not the only ones to do so. In the late seventies and early eighties, trapping for dollars became a popular pastime, as housewives, teenagers and retirees got into the act.

If the bobcat had been as difficult to lure into a steel jawed leghold trap as it is to observe, all this pressure on it would have presented no threat. The bobcat, however, is vulnerable in the extreme to trapping. Whereas a coyote reacts with suspicion to any novel object, the bobcat's feline nature compels it to investigate and play with every new thing. As a result, no special skill is required to catch it. It hardly matters what kind of bait is used. In times past, trappers often lamented the bobcat's tendency to get into traps they had scented to attract more valuable furbearers. By the early 1980s, however, finding a bobcat in a fox or badger set was cause for celebration. It is hardly surprising therefore that a good many people viewed the escalating pressure on this cat with some alarm.

"They're overtrapped," I was told by one veteran trapper of 50 years. "The price is too big. They don't propagate like coyotes, you know."

This man's knowledge of animals, gained from years in the field, squared with scientific evidence. The bobcat's reproductive rate is indeed low. Data collected in Wyoming by investigator Douglas Crowe demonstrate that a female bobcat produces but a single litter annually. Moreover, by counting placental scars in bobcat carcasses, Crowe established that the average number of embryos per litter is only 2.8. And, of course, not every incipient offspring comes to term.

Nor is kitten survival high. One explanation for this is that a mother bobcat, unlike a mother coyote or wolf, receives no help from her mate (or pack member) in rearing her family. And feeding a family of meat-eaters is not easy. Everybody's dinner must be stalked and captured—a demand on the mother that persists at gradually diminishing levels until her kittens are nine or ten months old. Furthermore, the bobcat never acquired the coyote's trick of toting food in her stomach and then regurgitating it at the den. Every weighty carcass must be dragged, often across long stretches of rough and broken country, to wherever her litter is stashed. And when rabbit populations are at a low ebb, a mother bobcat may have to travel far afield to make a kill. Given these difficulties, 2.8 embroyos probably represents the optimum number of kittens the mother bobcat has any chance of raising—and only in the best of years.

What all this adds up to is that the bobcat does not compensate for high mortality by producing larger litters. Unlike deer, mice or even coyotes, it is biologically incapable of doing so. For this reason, heavy trapping pressure could prove fatal to a population already depressed by natural factors. A case in point is the bobcat's nearest relative, the Canada lynx. Investigators Christopher Brand and Lloyd Keith demonstrated that in localities where lynx trapping was allowed to proceed during periods of snowshoe hare scarcity, the species did not make a comeback. Their study challenges a long-standing wildlife management assumption that trapping is always "compensatory"—meaning that where trapping is banned, other natural causes of death come into play to reduce the species to an equivalent level. Brand and Keith show that, in the case of the lynx, trapping mortality is actually "additive"—at least during years when snowshoe hares are in short supply, and they urged that trapping of lynx be curtailed during those times.*

But in the late 1970s and early 1980s no weight was given to such biological arguments. The bobcat existed to be exploited. How much money the species could bring in was the bottom line. No matter that the animal's range had shrunk dramatically. Once native to every one of the lower forty-eight states, it was now absent from wide swaths of the Midwest and East. In New Jersey it had been declared extinct and efforts were underway to restock it. Indiana, Iowa, Ohio and Delaware listed it as "endangered." Illinois called it "threatened." In Kentucky, Pennsylvania, Rhode Island and Maryland numbers were so low the animal was given total protection. Many other states, however, impressed by the animal's sudden worth, elevated it from the status of "varmint" to that of "furbearer" and set seasons when it might be trapped. Of the states where bobcats were being trapped, only nine imposed a bag limit and none placed a limit on licenses sold. Hence trapper numbers grew—in 1979–80 by 21 percent. Likewise the number of bobcat pelts exported to fur-hungry nations swelled. In 1980 the figure was 90,000.

What was happening to the bobcat was precisely what the

---

*An indicator of how vulnerable the bobcat may be is the fate of America's other native felines. Today the jaguar is extinct within our borders. The ocelot, the jaguarundi and the margay are so rare as to be invisible. The cougar or mountain lion can be regarded as viable only in a few regions of the West and with help may hang on in Florida. And the lynx, whose range borders Canada, has decreased to the vanishing point in New England and Wisconsin.

framers of the CITES Treaty had foreseen and tried to prevent. Mindful of the impact that a total embargo on endangered leopards, ocelots, margays, and cheetahs could have on other spotted cats, they placed the bobcat on a secondary list. Export of animals on this list was to be based on findings that such export was not harmful to the species. In the case of the secretive bobcat, however, no reliable census existed to establish how viable the species might or might not be.

At first a United States federal panel appointed to carry out this CITES proviso (the Endangered Species Scientific Authority or ESSA) responded properly. Lacking reliable population data on the bobcat, it announced a total ban on export of its pelt. For a brief period it appeared that a mechanism was in place to dampen exploitation of the species. And indeed that mechanism did work. Lacking a foreign outlet, pelt prices plummeted. Concurrently, however, a chorus of trapper complaints mounted. And joining their loud voices were those of the states' game and fish officials, whose coffers depend in some large measure on the sale of trapping licenses. They accused the federal government of usurping the states' authority over wildlife. As a result, within a few months the federal panel reversed itself and granted any state that initiated a tagging program the right to export bobcat pelts without limit. Of course, tagging programs were initiated everywhere, for whatever that was worth.

Meanwhile a number of surprised wildlife and humane organizations expressed their misgivings to ESSA. Their objections however, fell on deaf ears and, in the end, Defenders of Wildlife took legal steps to protect the bobcat. It went to court, charging ESSA with failure to abide by this country's treaty obligations. Defenders argued that the population figures given to ESSA by the states were not only unscientific, but failed to prove that export was not harming the species.

The lawsuit that ensued was protracted and bitterly contested not only by ESSA, but by the state fish and game agencies, as represented by the International Association of Fish and Wildlife Agencies or IAFWA. Several trapper associations and representatives from the fur industry also joined the case—siding with the defense, of course.

As formidable as was this alliance, in 1981 (two years, one appeal and perhaps a quarter of a million dead bobcats later) a U.S.

Court of Appeals handed down findings in favor of Defenders. According to the judge, the biological standards used by ESSA to authorize bobcat exports had indeed been "inadequate" and should be "set aside." The case was remanded to a lower court with instructions to favor protection of the animal where doubt existed.

What for one brief moment seemed certain victory for the bobcat, however, quickly evaporated, as attorneys for fur and trapping interests and for the state fish and game agencies worked to circumvent the judgment. Even while announcing their intention to take the case all the way to the U.S. Supreme Court, they convinced the International Convention Advisory Commission, a new panel named to supersede ESSA, to circulate a proposal to the 66 other signatories of the CITES Treaty asking that the bobcat be delisted. They also persuaded Louisiana Congressman John Breaux to tack a rider onto the Endangered Species Bill, which was up for reauthorization. That amendment would effectively render moot the court's findings regarding bobcat exports.

In the end Defenders, lacking the necessary support in Congress to kill the Breaux amendment, was forced to accept a weak compromise. The amendment was redrafted. Although it still contained language which relieved the states from having to account for their bobcat populations, it allowed that the International Convention Advisory Commission, in setting export quotas, could make use of bobcat population data, if such data was available. Case closed.

That was how it was for the bobcat in 1983. Now some seven years later, it still defies reason that state and federal agencies charged with the protection of our nation's wildlife should have been so resistant to giving the bobcat a break. In retrospect, however, it seems clear that what was at issue here was not the survival of the bobcat at all, but the survival of the undisputed authority that states exercise over wildlife. As for abiding by our treaty obligations, the United States presented two faces: one to Third World signatory nations who were asked to embargo their ivory and other animal products; the other to the American trapper whose right to make top money on bobcats was simply not open to question.

So how does the bobcat fare in 1990?

As incredible as it may seem, what could not be accomplished in the halls of Congress or by judicial action just might come about through public consciousness-raising. Anti-fur campaigns are having a dramatic effect on fur sales. Last year, New York's top three furriers reported significant losses and one of these giants had to file for bankruptcy after deep price slashing failed to rescue it. Weekly anti-fur demonstrations in New York City (where more than one-third of the nation's furs are marketed) has seen huge turnouts and the message conveyed has been loud and clear: fur is no longer smart or sexy. Much credit for this strategy is due People for Ethical Treatment of Animals or PETA, who masterminded a series of slick ad campaigns announcing that "Fur Is Dead" and who convinced a host of high profile glamour figures—such as Candice Bergen, Ali MacGraw, Bea Arthur and Carol Burnett—to go public in denouncing furs.

But even these achievements pale in the light of what is happening in Europe. One need only look to Holland, which has become virtually fur-free, to see what human education can accomplish. There only 32 of the nation's 400 fur stores have managed to keep their doors open in the face of a 90% decline in sales. In Great Britain and Switzerland, business is off by 75% from five years ago. And in West Germany, formerly a major bobcat market, figures show a 25% decline in fur purchases.

If the bottom hasn't fallen out of the fur-coat market, the top, sleeves and collars certainly have. Lacking a foreign outlet, middlemen are now paying trappers a pittance for their pelts. As a result, over the past two winters trapper fever has subsided. In the December 1989 issue of *Fur Fish and Game*, bobcat was listed as going for $20 to $40 a pelt—shades of 1970! At those prices, it likely costs a trapper more to tank up his pickup and go check his traplines than he can hope to realize from his labor. Obviously, without an overseas market, the wearing of bobcat is a fashion whose time has gone. Meanwhile the word is out that "fun furs" do not bring joy to sensitive people.

Sources

Allen, Durward. *Our Wildlife Legacy.* New York: Funk & Wagnalls, 1962.

Bailey, Theodore N. "Den Ecology and Adult-Young Relationships in Bobcats." Paper presented at the Bobcat Research Conference sponsored by the National Wildlife Federation and the Endangered Species Scientific Authority, Port Royal, Virginia, October 1979.

———. "Ecology of Bobcats with Special Reference to Social Organization." Ph.D. thesis, University of Idaho, 1972.

———. "The Elusive Bobcat." *Natural History,* October 1972.

———. "Marking Behavior." Ph.D. thesis, special appendix, University of Idaho, 1972.

———. "Mortality Patterns and Age-related Characteristics of Eastern Idaho Bobcats." Paper presented at the Bobcat Research Conference sponsored by the National Wildlife Federation and the Endangered Species Scientific Authority, Port Royal, Virginia, October 1979.

———. "Social Organization in a Bobcat Population." *Journal of Wildlife Management* 38 (1974): 435–46.

Beadle, Muriel. *The Cat.* New York: Simon & Schuster, 1977.

Bekoff, Marc. "The Development of Social Interaction, Play and Metacommunication in Mammals: An Ethological Perspective." *Quarterly Review of Biology* 47 (December 1972): 412–54.

Bobcat Research Conference Proceedings. Published in Washington, D.C., by National Wildlife Federation, 1981. Science and Technical Series #6.

Brand, Christopher J., and Keith, Lloyd B. "Lynx Demography During a Snowshoe Hare Decline in Alberta." *Journal of Wildlife Management* 43 (1979): 827–49.

Cahalane, Victor A. *Mammals of North America.* New York: Macmillan, 1961.

Crowe, Douglas M. "Aspects of Ageing, Growth and Reproduction of Bobcats from Wyoming." *Journal of Mammalogy* 56 (1975): 177–98.

Crowe, Douglas M. "A Model for Exploited Bobcat Populations in Wyoming." *Journal of Wildlife Management* 39 (1975): 408–15.

Eaton, Randall L. "Group Interaction, Spacing and Territoriality in Cheetahs." *Z Tierpsychol.* 27 (1970): 481–91.

———, ed. *The World's Cats*, vol. 1: *Ecology and Conservation.* Proceedings of an International Symposium, Winston, Oregon, May 1973, published by World Wildlife Safari.

———, ed. *The World's Cats*, vol. 2: *Behavior and Management of Reproduction.* Proceedings of an International Symposium, Winston, Oregon, May 1973, published by World Wildlife Safari.

Fox, Michael W. "Socio-infantile and Socio-sexual Signals in Canids: A Comparative and Developmental Study." *Behavior* 35 (1971): 242–58.

———. *Understanding Your Cat.* New York: Coward, McCann & Geoghegan, 1974.

Gilbert, Bil. *The Weasels.* New York: Pantheon, 1970.

Grosvenor, Melville Bell. *Wild Animals of North America.* Washington, D.C.: National Geographic Society, 1960.

Guggisberg, C. A. W. *Wild Cats of the World.* New York: Taplinger, 1975.

Hall, E. Raymond. Correspondence containing updated material on subspeciation of *Lynx rufus* June 9, 1979.

Hall, E. Raymond. "Defenders of Wildlife v. Endangered Species Scientific Authority." Testimony on differentiation of nine subspecies of *Lynx rufus* in the United States. Affidavit for plaintiff in U.S. District Court for Washington, D.C., 1979.

Hall, E. Raymond, and Kelson, Keith R. *The Mammals of North America.* New York: The Ronald Press Company, 1959.

Hornocker, M. G. "Winter Territoriality in Mountain Lions." *Journal of Wildlife Management* 33 (1969): 457–64.

Ipsen, D. C. *Rattlesnakes and Scientists.* Reading, Mass.: Addison-Wesley, 1970.

Jones, J. Knox, Carter, Dilford C., and Genoways, Hugh H. "Revised Checklist of North American Mammals North of Mexico." *Occasional Papers The Museum of Texas Tech University* #28, March 7, 1975.

Jorgensen, S. E., and Mech, L. David, eds. Proceedings of a symposium on *The Native Cats of North America: Their Status and Management.* Thirty-sixth North American Wildlife and Resources Conference, Portland, Oregon, March 9, 1971.

Kasendorf, Jeanie. "The Fur Flies." *New York.* January 15, 1990.

Keith, L. B. *Wildlife's Ten Year Cycle.* Madison, Wisc.: University of Wisconsin Press, 1963.

Kleiman, D. G., and Eisenberg, J. F. "Comparisons of Canid and Felid Social Systems from an Evolutionary Perspective." *Animal Behavior* 21 (1973): 637–59.

Leyhausen, Paul. *Cat Behavior.* New York: Garland Press, 1977.

Lorenz, K., and Leyhausen, P. *Motivation of Human and Animal Behavior.* New York: Van Nostrand Reinhold, 1973.

Nellis, Carl H., Wetmore, Stephen P., and Keith, Lloyd B. "Lynx-Prey Interaction in Central Alberta." *Journal of Wildlife Management* 36 (1972): 320–29.

Pond, Grace, and Sayer, Angela. *The Intelligent Cat.* New York: Dial Press, 1977.

Ryden, Hope. *God's Dog: A Celebration of the North American Coyote.* New York: The Viking Press, 1978.

Schroeder, Gary. *Fur Fish and Game.* December 1989.

Tomkies, Mike. *My Wilderness Wildcats.* New York: Doubleday, 1978.

Van Wormer, Joe. *The World of the Bobcat.* New York: Lippincott, 1963.